Myths From Wales

ISBN: 9798332762697

www.TarversGuides.com

Contents:

The Enchanting World of Welsh Mythology

Welsh mythology is a treasure trove of captivating tales that have been passed down through generations. These stories, rich in symbolism and wonder, offer a glimpse into the beliefs, values, and imagination of the ancient Welsh people. From shape-shifting wizards to heroic kings, from otherworldly creatures to legendary quests, Welsh myths have enthralled listeners and readers for centuries.

The roots of Welsh mythology stretch back to the Iron Age, intertwining with the broader Celtic traditions of Britain and Ireland. As the Romans withdrew from Britain in the 5th century, leaving the island to face waves of Anglo-Saxon invaders, the Welsh people clung to their distinct cultural identity. Their myths and legends became a powerful tool for preserving their heritage and making sense of a changing world.

Many of these stories were passed down orally by bards and storytellers known as cyfarwyddiaid. These skilled wordsmiths played a crucial role in Welsh society, not just as entertainers but as keepers of history and tradition. They wove tales of gods and heroes, of magical lands and fierce battles, each story a thread in the tapestry of Welsh culture.

It wasn't until the Middle Ages that many of these oral traditions were written down. The most famous collection is the Mabinogion, a group of eleven prose stories compiled from medieval Welsh manuscripts. These tales, along with other sources like the Welsh Triads and the work of medieval historians, form the core of what we now know as Welsh mythology.

Welsh myths often feature a cast of memorable characters. Gods and goddesses like Rhiannon and Arianrhod, heroes like Culhwch and Pwyll, and wizards like Gwydion and Merlin (or Myrddin in Welsh) populate these stories. The myths also introduce us to unique supernatural creatures such as the Cŵn Annwn (spectral hounds) and the Tylwyth Teg (fair folk or fairies).

These stories aren't just entertaining tales; they're windows into the Welsh worldview. They reflect the importance of honour, the power of magic, the beauty of the natural world, and the complex relationships between mortals and divine beings. They speak of a land where the boundary between our world and the Otherworld is thin, where magic and reality intertwine.

Welsh mythology has had a lasting impact on literature and popular culture. It has influenced writers from Geoffrey of Monmouth in the 12th century to modern fantasy authors. The Arthurian legends, which have captured imaginations worldwide, have strong roots in Welsh tradition.

Today, these myths continue to resonate. They remind us of our connection to the natural world, the power of storytelling, and the enduring human need for wonder and magic. As you delve into the chapters that follow, prepare to be transported to a world of enchantment, where anything is possible and where ancient wisdom still speaks to us across the centuries.

Cŵn Annwn

In the enchanting hills and valleys of Wales, where ancient tales whisper on the wind, there's a story that sends shivers down the spine of even the bravest souls. It's the legend of the Cŵn Annwn, the spectral hounds of the otherworld. These are no ordinary dogs, mind you, but ghostly creatures that roam the night, their howls a haunting reminder of the thin veil between our world and the next.

The Tale of Cŵn Annwn

Picture a moonlit night in the Welsh countryside. The air is crisp, and a fog rolls in from the hills. Suddenly, a sound breaks the silence - a distant baying that seems to come from everywhere and nowhere at once. It's the Cŵn Annwn, the hounds of Annwn, on their otherworldly hunt.

These spectral hounds are not of our world. They come from Annwn, the otherworld in Welsh mythology, a place of wonder and mystery. The Cŵn Annwn are no ordinary pack of dogs. Their coats are as white as freshly fallen snow, gleaming with an unearthly light. But it's their ears that truly set them apart - bright red, like the colour of fresh blood, a stark contrast to their pale fur.

Leading this ghostly pack is none other than Arawn, the king of Annwn himself. He rides through the night sky, his dark cloak billowing behind him as he urges his hounds onward.

Sometimes, he's joined by Mallt-y-Nos, a fearsome hag who adds her own chilling cries to the cacophony of the hunt.

The Cŵn Annwn don't hunt for sport or food. Their prey are the souls of wrongdoers, those who have committed evil deeds in life. As they chase these unfortunate spirits across the sky, their howls grow louder and more frenzied. But here's the strange thing - the closer they get to their quarry, the quieter their growls become. It's said that when the Cŵn Annwn fall silent, death is near.

Folks in Wales knew to be wary when they heard the sound of the Wild Hunt. It was most active on certain eve nights, particularly in autumn and winter when the nights grew long and dark. The howling of the Cŵn Annwn was a sure sign that someone nearby would soon pass away.

But not everyone recognised the sound for what it was. Some mistook the eerie cries of the Cŵn Annwn for the honking of migrating geese. Perhaps it was easier to believe in birds than in supernatural hounds. Still, those who knew the old stories understood the true nature of those sounds echoing across the hills.

The Cŵn Annwn weren't just harbingers of doom, though. They also had the important job of escorting souls to the Otherworld. Like ghostly sheepdogs, they would round up the spirits of the recently departed and guide them on their final journey.

As Christianity spread through Wales, the story of the Cŵn

Annwn took on new meanings. Some began to call them "The Hounds of Hell", imagining Annwn not as the paradise it was in Welsh tradition, but as a place of punishment. Yet for those who remembered the old ways, the Cŵn Annwn remained creatures of mystery and wonder, neither good nor evil, but simply part of the natural order of things.

And so, on dark nights in Wales, when the wind howls and strange sounds echo in the distance, some still wonder - could that be the Cŵn Annwn on their endless hunt?

The tale of the Cŵn Annwn is deeply rooted in Welsh mythology and folklore, reflecting the rich cultural heritage of this ancient land. To understand the significance of these spectral hounds, we need to delve into the beliefs and traditions of the Welsh people.

Wales has a long history of Celtic influence, and the Cŵn Annwn story is a prime example of Celtic mythology. The concept of an otherworld, Annwn, is central to many Welsh tales. It's not seen as a place of punishment like the Christian hell, but rather as a parallel realm of magic and wonder.

The figure of Arawn, the king of Annwn, appears in several Welsh myths. He's a complex character, sometimes portrayed as a friend to mortals, other times as a fearsome ruler of the dead. His role as the leader of the Wild Hunt with the Cŵn Annwn shows his connection to both life and death.

The Wild Hunt itself is a motif that appears in various

European mythologies, not just in Wales. It usually involves a ghostly or supernatural group of hunters passing in wild pursuit across the sky. The leader of the hunt varies depending on the culture, but the basic idea remains the same - it's a terrifying spectacle that mortals should avoid at all costs.

In Wales, the Wild Hunt became closely associated with the Cŵn Annwn. This connection likely developed over centuries, blending older Celtic beliefs with newer folklore. The hounds' role in hunting down wrongdoers might reflect a societal need for justice, even after death.

The description of the Cŵn Annwn, with their white coats and red ears, is significant in Celtic symbolism. White is often associated with the otherworld and supernatural beings in Celtic lore. The red ears, meanwhile, are a common feature of magical or otherworldly animals in Welsh and Irish myths. Red is frequently linked to death and the otherworld in Celtic traditions.

As Christianity spread through Wales, it inevitably influenced how people viewed these old stories. The reframing of Annwn as a hellish place, and the Cŵn Annwn as "Hounds of Hell", shows how new religious ideas were grafted onto existing beliefs. This process, where old myths are reinterpreted through a new cultural lens, is common in many societies.

The connection between the Cŵn Annwn and death omens reflects the Welsh people's attempts to understand and predict death. In a time before modern medicine, when life was often short and unpredictable, such beliefs provided a way to make sense of mortality.

It's worth noting that the Cŵn Annwn aren't always portrayed negatively. Their role in escorting souls to the otherworld suggests they were also seen as guides or protectors. This dual nature - frightening yet potentially helpful - is typical of many supernatural beings in folklore.

The persistence of the Cŵn Annwn legend over centuries speaks to its deep roots in Welsh culture. Even as society changed and new ideas came in, the image of these spectral hounds continued to capture people's imaginations.

Etymology and Symbolism

The name "Cŵn Annwn" itself is packed with meaning. In Welsh, "cŵn" simply means "dogs" or "hounds". "Annwn" is the name of the otherworld in Welsh mythology. So, literally, the name means "Hounds of Annwn" or "Hounds of the Otherworld".

The concept of Annwn is crucial to understanding these hounds. In Welsh myth, Annwn isn't a place of punishment like the Christian hell. Instead, it's often described as a wonderful realm, sometimes even called the "Court of Intoxication". It's a place of eternal youth, beauty, and abundance. This positive view of the otherworld makes the Cŵn Annwn more complex than simple "hellhounds".

The physical description of the Cŵn Annwn is rich in symbolism. Their white coats represent their otherworldly nature. In many cultures, white is associated with ghosts, spirits, and the supernatural. It's the colour of the moon, which is often linked to magic and mystery.

The red ears of the Cŵn Annwn are particularly significant. In Celtic mythology, red ears are a common feature of supernatural animals. They're seen as a mark of the otherworld. Red is also associated with blood and, by extension, with life and death. The contrast between the white coats and red ears creates a striking image that emphasises the hounds' supernatural nature.

The quietening of the hounds' growls as they approach their prey is an interesting detail. It goes against what we'd expect - normally, dogs get louder as they get closer to what they're chasing. This reversal adds to the otherworldly feel of the Cŵn Annwn. It also creates a chilling effect - the silence becomes more frightening than the noise.

The association of the Cŵn Annwn with geese is intriguing. Geese are migratory birds, moving between places just as the hounds move between worlds. In many cultures, birds are seen as messengers between the world of the living and the world of the dead. This connection might have made it easier for people to link the sound of geese with the mythical hounds.

Superstitions and Beliefs

The legend of the Cŵn Annwn gave rise to various superstitions and beliefs in Wales. Here are some of the most notable ones:

• Death Omen: The howling of the Cŵn Annwn was widely

believed to be a portent of death. If someone heard the hounds, it was thought that a death would soon occur in the area.

• Seasonal Activity: The Cŵn Annwn were believed to be most active during autumn and winter, particularly on certain eve nights. This could be linked to the Celtic calendar, where winter was associated with the otherworld.

• Protective Measures: Some people believed that staying indoors on nights when the Wild Hunt was active could protect them from the Cŵn Annwn.

• Soul Guides: Despite their fearsome reputation, the Cŵn Annwn were also believed to guide souls to the otherworld. This gave them a more positive role as psychopomps, or soul guides.

• Justice After Death: The belief that the Cŵn Annwn hunted down wrongdoers suggested a form of cosmic justice. It implied that even after death, one couldn't escape the consequences of evil deeds.

• Transformation of Beliefs: As Christianity spread, some people began to view the Cŵn Annwn as demons or associates of the devil. This shows how older beliefs can be reinterpreted through new religious lenses.

These superstitions reflect the deep impact the Cŵn Annwn had on Welsh folklore and the way people understood death and the afterlife.

The legend of the Cŵn Annwn isn't unique to Wales. Similar stories of spectral hounds can be found across the British Isles and beyond. This suggests a common cultural thread running through these regions, possibly dating back to ancient Celtic or even pre-Celtic times.

In England, we find tales of the Gabriel Hounds and the Wisht Hounds of Dartmoor. These ghostly packs are also associated with the Wild Hunt and are said to foretell death or disaster. The similarity to the Cŵn Annwn is striking, suggesting a shared origin or at least significant cultural exchange.

Scotland has its own version in the Cu Sith, a giant, green fairy dog said to hunt in the Highlands. Like the Cŵn Annwn, the Cu Sith is associated with the otherworld and death.

In Norse mythology, we find Odin leading the Wild Hunt with his own pack of hounds. This parallel shows how widespread the concept of supernatural hounds and celestial hunts was across Northern Europe.

The idea of dogs as guardians of the underworld goes back even further. In Greek mythology, we have Cerberus, the three-headed dog guarding the entrance to Hades. While not directly related to the Cŵn Annwn, it shows a long-standing association between dogs and the realm of the dead in European mythology.

The Cŵn Annwn's role as soul guides also has parallels in other cultures. In ancient Egypt, for example, Anubis, the jackal-headed god, was responsible for guiding souls to the afterlife. While the details differ, the basic concept of canine figures assisting in the journey after death is similar.

These connections show how the story of the Cŵn Annwn fits into a broader tapestry of mythological traditions. While uniquely Welsh in its specifics, it shares themes and motifs with legends from around the world.

The Cŵn Annwn in Welsh Landscape and Culture

The legend of the Cŵn Annwn is deeply intertwined with the Welsh landscape. The misty hills, deep valleys, and ancient forests of Wales provide the perfect backdrop for tales of supernatural hounds.

Many specific locations in Wales are associated with sightings or tales of the Cŵn Annwn. For example, the Black Mountains in south-east Wales are said to be a favourite hunting ground for the spectral pack. The remote and rugged nature of this area lends itself well to stories of otherworldly encounters.

The Cŵn Annwn have also left their mark on Welsh place names. For instance, there's a mountain pass in Snowdonia called Bwlch y Cŵn, which means "Pass of the Dogs". While this might refer to ordinary dogs, some link it to legends of the Cŵn Annwn.

In Welsh literature, the Cŵn Annwn appear in several important works. They're mentioned in the Mabinogion, a collection of Welsh prose stories compiled in the Middle Ages. This shows how central these hounds were to Welsh storytelling traditions.

Even today, the legend of the Cŵn Annwn continues to inspire Welsh culture. They appear in modern Welsh literature, art, and even music. Some Welsh bands have written songs about these spectral hounds, keeping the legend alive for new generations.

The Cŵn Annwn also play a role in Welsh tourism. Ghost tours and storytelling events often feature tales of these supernatural hounds, attracting visitors interested in Welsh folklore and the paranormal.

In this way, the Cŵn Annwn remain an important part of Welsh cultural identity. They connect modern Wales to its mythical past, reminding people of the rich folklore that's woven into the very landscape of the country.

The tale of the Cŵn Annwn is more than just a spooky story. It's a window into the beliefs, fears, and hopes of generations of Welsh people. These spectral hounds embody the mystery of death and the unknown, the idea of justice beyond the grave, and the enduring connection between our world and the otherworld.

The persistence of this legend over centuries shows its deep roots in Welsh culture. Even as society has changed, the image of the white hounds with red ears continues to capture the imagination. It reminds us of the power of folklore to shape how we see the world around us.

In the end, the Cŵn Annwn are more than just characters in an old tale. They're a part of Wales itself, as much a feature of the landscape as the mountains and valleys. Their howls echo through Welsh history, connecting the present to a rich mythological past. As long as people tell stories on dark Welsh nights, the Cŵn Annwn will continue their eternal hunt across the skies of Wales.

Gwydion

In the misty hills and verdant valleys of Wales, tales of magic and wonder have been whispered for centuries. Among these stories, one figure looms large: Gwydion fab Dôn, a powerful magician, cunning trickster, and legendary hero. His tale is woven into the very fabric of Welsh mythology, a tapestry of adventure, deceit, and transformation that has captivated generations.

The Tale of Gwydion: The Magician of Welsh Mythology

Long ago, in the land of Wales, there lived a magician of great renown named Gwydion. He was the son of Dôn, a figure of divine origin, and his powers were said to be unmatched throughout the land. Gwydion's home was in Gwynedd, in the north of Wales, where the mountains touch the sky and the forests whisper ancient secrets.

One day, Gwydion heard tell of magical pigs in the south, owned by Pryderi, the king of Dyfed. These were no ordinary swine, but creatures of great value and power. Gwydion, ever the trickster, hatched a plan to steal these pigs for his own kingdom.

With clever words and magical illusions, Gwydion tricked Pryderi into trading the pigs for horses and dogs that were nothing more than enchanted mushrooms and leaves. When the illusion faded, Pryderi was furious and declared war on Gwynedd.

The war raged across the land, and in the end, Gwydion faced Pryderi in single combat. With his superior magic and cunning, Gwydion emerged victorious, and Pryderi lay slain.

But Gwydion's victory came at a great cost. While he was away at war, a terrible crime had been committed by his brother Gilfaethwy. In Welsh mythology, Math fab Mathonwy, the king of Gwynedd, had a unique condition - he needed to have his feet held in the lap of a virgin at all times, except during war, or he would die. Goewin was the young woman who held this important role of "foot-holder" for Math. Taking advantage of Math's absence during the war, Gilfaethwy had raped Goewin. When Math returned and learned of this heinous act, he was furious with both Gwydion and Gilfaethwy for their roles in this deception and crime.

As punishment, Math used his own powerful magic to transform Gwydion and Gilfaethwy into animals. For three years, they lived as different pairs of animals – first as deer, then as wild pigs, and finally as wolves. Each year, they bore offspring which became human and were raised by Math.

After their punishment, Gwydion sought to make amends. He suggested his sister, Arianrhod, as the new foot-holder for Math. But when Arianrhod stepped over Math's magical staff, she gave birth to two children, revealing she was not a virgin.

One child, Dylan, immediately fled to the sea. The other was taken by Gwydion, who raised him as his own son. This child would become Lleu Llaw Gyffes, a hero in his own right.

Arianrhod, shamed and angry, placed three curses on her son. She swore he would never have a name, never bear arms, and never have a human wife. But Gwydion, with his clever magic and quick wit, overcame each curse in turn.

To give Lleu a name, Gwydion disguised himself and Lleu as shoemakers. When Arianrhod came to have shoes made, Lleu struck a bird with a stone so accurately that Arianrhod exclaimed, "The fair-haired one has a skilful hand!" Thus, Lleu Llaw Gyffes ("Fair-Haired One with the Skilful Hand") was named.

To arm Lleu, Gwydion created an illusion of an attacking fleet, causing Arianrhod to arm them both in defense. And finally, to give Lleu a wife, Gwydion and Math created a woman from flowers, naming her Blodeuwedd.

But Gwydion's greatest test was yet to come. Blodeuwedd betrayed Lleu, conspiring with her lover to kill him. Lleu was struck with a spear and transformed into an eagle. For a year, Gwydion searched for his son, finally finding him perched in a great oak tree.

With a song of magic, Gwydion lured Lleu down and restored him to human form. He then pursued justice, turning Blodeuwedd into an owl as punishment for her betrayal.

In his final great feat, Gwydion fought in the Battle of the Trees against Arawn, king of the otherworld. With his knowledge of magic and nature, Gwydion identified the enchanted warrior Bran among Arawn's forces, leading to victory for his side.

Throughout his many adventures, Gwydion proved himself to be not just a powerful magician, but a complex figure – capable of both great deeds and terrible mistakes, of cunning trickery and profound love. His tale remains a cornerstone of Welsh mythology, a story of magic, transformation, and the enduring power of wit and wisdom.

Historical Context and Origins

The tale of Gwydion is deeply rooted in Welsh mythology and folklore. His stories are primarily found in the Fourth Branch of the Mabinogi, a collection of Welsh prose stories compiled in the 12th or 13th century. However, references to Gwydion can be found in other medieval Welsh texts as well, including the Welsh Triads, the Book of Taliesin, and the Stanzas of the Graves.

The Mabinogi, including Gwydion's tale, was likely compiled from older oral traditions. These stories reflect the beliefs, values, and social structures of medieval Welsh society. They often blend elements of pre-Christian Celtic mythology with newer Christian influences, creating a unique tapestry of Welsh cultural heritage.

Gwydion's character embodies several important aspects of Welsh mythology:

1. The power of magic and transformation
2. The importance of cunning and wit
3. The complex relationships between gods, humans, and nature

4. The consequences of one's actions, both good and bad

His role as both a trickster and a hero reflects the Welsh appreciation for cleverness and the ability to overcome challenges through wit rather than brute force. This aligns with other trickster figures in world mythology, such as Loki in Norse myths or Anansi in African folklore.

The setting of Gwydion's tales in Gwynedd, a kingdom in North Wales, reflects the political landscape of medieval Wales. The conflict between Gwynedd and Dyfed (Pryderi's kingdom) mirrors the real-life tensions and rivalries between Welsh kingdoms during this period.

The magical elements in Gwydion's story, such as shape-shifting and creating life from flowers, have roots in ancient Celtic beliefs about the interconnectedness of all things and the power of druids or magicians to manipulate natural forces.

Etymology and Symbolism

The name Gwydion itself is rich with meaning. It's often interpreted as "Born of Trees" or "Son of the Wood," which ties into his connection with nature and magic. This etymology reflects the importance of trees in Celtic mythology, where they were often seen as sacred and imbued with magical properties.

Several symbolic elements appear throughout Gwydion's tales:

1. Animals: The transformation of Gwydion and his brother into animals reflects the belief in the interconnectedness of

humans and nature. Each animal (deer, pig, wolf) has its own symbolic meanings in Celtic lore.

2. Trees: The Battle of the Trees and Gwydion's name both highlight the importance of trees in Welsh mythology. Trees were often seen as gateways between worlds or sources of wisdom.

3. Flowers: The creation of Blodeuwedd from flowers symbolizes the power of nature and magic to create life. It also reflects the Welsh connection between women and flowers in mythology.

4. The Otherworld: The battle with Arawn, king of the otherworld, represents the thin veil between the mortal world and the supernatural realm in Welsh beliefs.

Superstitions and Beliefs

While there aren't many specific superstitions directly tied to Gwydion, his stories reflect several beliefs common in Welsh folklore:

1. The power of words: Gwydion's ability to overcome Arianrhod's curses through clever wordplay reflects the belief in the magical power of language.

2. Shape-shifting: The ability of gods and magic users to change their form or the form of others was a common belief.

3. The danger of the Otherworld: Interactions with beings from the Otherworld, like the battle with Arawn, were seen as

perilous but potentially rewarding.

4. The sacredness of oaths: The binding nature of Arianrhod's curses reflects the importance placed on sworn words in Welsh society.

Connections to Other Myths

Gwydion's character and stories share similarities with figures from other mythologies:

1. Like the Greek god Hermes or the Norse god Loki, Gwydion is a trickster figure who uses his wit to achieve his goals.

2. His role as a magician is similar to Merlin in Arthurian legends, another figure from British mythology known for his magical prowess.

3. The creation of Blodeuwedd from flowers is reminiscent of the Greek myth of Pygmalion, where a sculptor creates a woman from ivory.

4. The Battle of the Trees has parallels in Irish mythology, where trees are also animated for battle in some tales.

Gwydion in Welsh Astronomy

Interestingly, Gwydion's influence extends beyond earthly tales into the heavens. In Welsh tradition, the Milky Way is known as Caer Gwydion, or "The Castle of Gwydion." This celestial connection further emphasises Gwydion's importance in Welsh culture and his association with cosmic forces.

Gwydion's tales, with their mix of magic, trickery, and transformation, continue to captivate audiences today. They offer a window into the rich cultural heritage of Wales, reflecting the values, beliefs, and imagination of the Welsh people throughout history. From the misty mountains of Gwynedd to the starry expanse of Caer Gwydion, the legacy of this complex and fascinating figure lives on, a testament to the enduring power of Welsh mythology.

Dewi Sant

In the rolling hills of southwest Wales, where mist clings to the valleys and ancient stones whisper tales of old, there lived a man whose legacy would shape the spiritual heart of a nation. This is the story of Dewi Sant, better known to many as Saint David, the patron saint of Wales. His life, steeped in miracles and piety, has become a cornerstone of Welsh identity and Christian faith.

The Tale of Dewi San

Long ago, in the 6th century, a child was born to Sant, a prince of Ceredigion, and Non, a nun. Legend says that Non gave birth to Dewi on a clifftop during a fierce storm, and at the moment of his birth, a bolt of lightning struck the rock, splitting it in two. A spring of pure water gushed forth from the earth, marking the spot as blessed.

From his earliest days, Dewi was destined for greatness. He was educated at a monastery and became a priest, dedicating his life to God and to spreading the Christian faith throughout Wales. Dewi was known for his simple lifestyle and his devotion to hard work. He and his followers ploughed the fields without the help of animals, drinking only water and eating only bread with herbs and salt.

As Dewi's reputation for holiness grew, so did tales of his miracles. One of the most famous occurred at the Synod of

Brefi. As Dewi preached to a large crowd, some complained they couldn't hear him. Suddenly, the ground beneath his feet rose up, forming a small hill so that everyone could see and hear him clearly. A white dove, sent by God, was said to have settled on his shoulder as he spoke.

Dewi founded many churches and monasteries across Wales and beyond, including his own monastery at Glyn Rhosyn (now St Davids). Here, he established a strict ascetic rule known as the "Monastic Rule of David". Monks had to pull the plough themselves without draught animals; to drink only water; to eat only bread with salt and herbs; and to spend the evenings in prayer, reading and writing.

As he grew older, Dewi's holiness and wisdom became renowned throughout the Celtic world. On his deathbed, surrounded by his loyal monks, he uttered his famous last words: "Be joyful, keep the faith, and do the little things that you have heard and seen me do." With these words, Dewi passed away on March 1st, 589 AD.

Historical Context and Origins

The story of Dewi Sant is deeply rooted in the early Christian history of Wales. The 6th century was a time of great change in Britain. The Roman Empire had withdrawn its forces, leaving the island vulnerable to invasions from Anglo-Saxons. In this tumultuous period, Christianity played a crucial role in preserving Welsh culture and identity.

Dewi lived during what is often called the Age of Saints in Wales. This era saw the establishment of many monastic communities that became centres of learning and spirituality. These monasteries were instrumental in preserving Welsh language and culture in the face of Anglo-Saxon expansion.

While many of the details of Dewi's life are shrouded in legend, there is historical evidence of his existence. The earliest written account of his life comes from Rhygyfarch, a Welsh bishop who wrote a Latin biography of Dewi around 1090 AD. This work, while embellished with miraculous tales, is believed to be based on earlier sources and oral traditions.

Dewi's influence extended beyond Wales. He is said to have travelled to Jerusalem and Rome, and founded monasteries in Brittany. His monastery at St Davids became an important pilgrimage site, with Pope Calixtus II declaring in 1123 that two pilgrimages to St Davids were equal to one to Rome.

Etymology and Symbolism

The name 'Dewi' is the Welsh form of 'David', derived from the Hebrew name meaning 'beloved'. 'Sant' is Welsh for 'saint', so 'Dewi Sant' simply means 'Saint David'.

Symbolically, Dewi is often associated with the leek and the dove. The leek became a Welsh national symbol after Dewi reportedly advised Welsh warriors to wear leeks in their helmets to distinguish themselves from Saxon enemies. The dove represents the Holy Spirit and is linked to the miracle at the Synod of Brefi.

The rising of the ground beneath Dewi's feet symbolises his elevated spiritual status and his role in bringing the word of

God to the people. His ascetic lifestyle, emphasising hard work and simple living, became a model for monastic life in Wales and beyond.

Superstitions and Beliefs

Many superstitions and beliefs have grown up around Dewi Sant over the centuries. Some people believe that carrying a leek on St David's Day (March 1st) will bring good luck. Others say that if you stand on the spot where Dewi was born on a clear night, you might see the Milky Way pointing directly to St Davids Cathedral.

In some parts of Wales, it's said that the ghost of Dewi appears on stormy nights, guiding lost travellers to safety. Farmers have long believed that invoking Dewi's name while planting crops will ensure a good harvest.

There's also a tradition that Dewi's blessing can cure illnesses. Pilgrims still visit St Davids Cathedral hoping for miraculous healings, often leaving offerings at his shrine.

Connections to Other Myths

The story of Dewi Sant shares similarities with other saints' tales from the Celtic world. Like St Patrick in Ireland and St Columba in Scotland, Dewi is credited with spreading Christianity and founding numerous churches and monasteries.

The miracle of the ground rising beneath Dewi's feet is reminiscent of stories about other saints and holy figures. In Irish mythology, the hill of Tara is said to have risen up beneath the High Kings of Ireland during their coronation ceremonies.

The association of Dewi with a dove echoes Biblical imagery, particularly the baptism of Jesus where the Holy Spirit descended like a dove. This symbolism is found in many Christian traditions worldwide.

Dewi Sant in Welsh Culture

Dewi Sant's influence on Welsh culture cannot be overstated. March 1st, the anniversary of his death, is celebrated as St David's Day and is the national day of Wales. On this day, many Welsh people wear leeks or daffodils, eat traditional Welsh foods like cawl (a hearty soup) and Welsh cakes, and participate in parades and eisteddfodau (festivals of music and poetry).

St Davids, the smallest city in Britain, has become a major pilgrimage and tourist site. The cathedral built over Dewi's monastery is a testament to his enduring legacy. Schools, hospitals, and churches across Wales bear his name, keeping his memory alive in everyday Welsh life.

Dewi's last words, "Do the little things", have become a popular Welsh motto, encapsulating the saint's emphasis on carrying out small acts of kindness and living a good life through everyday actions.

The story of Dewi Sant is more than just a religious tale. It's a narrative that has helped shape Welsh identity for over a thousand years. In Dewi, the Welsh found a figure who embodied their values of hard work, simplicity, and devotion. His life and teachings continue to inspire people in Wales and beyond, serving as a bridge between ancient traditions and modern Welsh culture. Whether seen as a historical figure or a legendary saint, Dewi Sant remains at the heart of what it means to be Welsh.

The Hunt of Twrch Trwyth

In the misty hills and valleys of ancient Wales, where myth and reality often blurred, there once roamed a creature of terrible power and fearsome reputation. This was no ordinary beast, but the legendary boar known as Twrch Trwyth. His tale is one of transformation, pursuit, and the heroic deeds of King Arthur and his brave companions.

The Tale of Twrch Trwyth

Long ago, in the green lands of Wales, there lived a prince who, through dark magic or divine punishment, was transformed into a monstrous boar. This creature, now known as Twrch Trwyth, was no ordinary swine. He stood taller than a man, with bristles as sharp as spears and tusks that could gore the mightiest warrior.

Twrch Trwyth's legend became entwined with the story of Culhwch, a young man seeking to win the hand of the fair Olwen. Olwen's father, the giant Ysbaddaden, set Culhwch a series of impossible tasks, one of which was to retrieve a comb, razor, and shears from between the ears of Twrch Trwyth.

Knowing he couldn't face such a beast alone, Culhwch turned to his cousin, the great King Arthur, for help. Arthur, always ready for adventure, gathered his bravest knights and finest hounds, including his loyal dog Cafall.

The hunt began in Ireland, where Twrch Trwyth had been

causing havoc. As Arthur and his men approached, the great boar sensed danger and fled across the sea to Wales. The chase was on, with Twrch Trwyth leading Arthur's party on a wild pursuit across the Welsh countryside.

Through forests and over mountains they raced, the boar's strength seeming endless. Wherever Twrch Trwyth passed, he left destruction in his wake. Crops were trampled, villages destroyed, and brave warriors were gored by his fearsome tusks.

Arthur's men used all their skill and cunning to corner the beast. They drove him from county to county, from Dyfed to Ceredigion, and on to Powys. At every turn, Twrch Trwyth fought back fiercely, his venomous bristles injuring many of Arthur's hounds and warriors.

Finally, after a chase that had lasted days, they cornered Twrch Trwyth in Cornwall. Here, in a final desperate battle, Arthur's men managed to snatch the comb, razor, and shears from between the boar's ears. But even in defeat, Twrch Trwyth would not be captured. With a mighty leap, the great boar plunged into the sea and disappeared beneath the waves, never to be seen again.

Historical Context and Origins

The tale of Twrch Trwyth is deeply rooted in Welsh mythology and Arthurian legend. It appears in its most detailed form in the Welsh prose romance "Culhwch and Olwen," which was written down around 1100 AD. However, the story's origins likely stretch back much further into Welsh oral tradition.

The boar hunt itself has earlier roots, appearing in a simpler form in the ninth-century "Historia Brittonum." This earlier version mentions Arthur hunting a boar called 'Troynt,' likely an early form of Twrch Trwyth's name. It's in this text that we first hear of Arthur's dog leaving its pawprint on a stone during the chase, a detail that would be expanded in later tellings.

The elaborate hunt described in "Culhwch and Olwen" reflects the importance of hunting in medieval Welsh society. Hunting was not just a sport for the nobility, but a crucial skill for survival and a test of bravery and leadership. The tale of Twrch Trwyth elevates this familiar activity to mythic proportions, turning a boar hunt into an epic quest involving magic, transformation, and heroic deeds.

The story also showcases the landscape of Wales, with the chase taking Arthur and his men across recognisable regions of the country. This grounding in real geography helps to root the mythical tale in the physical world, making it feel more immediate and real to its audience.

Etymology and Symbolism

The name Twrch Trwyth itself is full of meaning. 'Twrch' in Welsh simply means 'wild boar,' while 'Trwyth' has been the subject of much scholarly debate. Some link it to the Irish word 'triath,' meaning 'king,' which would fit with the idea of Twrch Trwyth as a transformed prince. Others see connections to words meaning 'royal' or 'kingly' in various Celtic languages.

Symbolically, the boar held great significance in Celtic culture. It was seen as a creature of strength, courage, and ferocity - qualities highly valued in warriors. The transformation of a prince into a boar could thus be seen as emphasising these warrior-like qualities, albeit in a monstrous form.

The items sought from Twrch Trwyth - the comb, razor, and shears - also carry symbolic weight. These grooming implements, associated with civilised behaviour, contrast sharply with the wild, bestial nature of the boar. Their placement between the boar's ears, the seat of thought and reason, further emphasises this clash between human and animal natures.

Superstitions and Beliefs

The tale of Twrch Trwyth taps into several superstitions and beliefs common in medieval Wales. The idea of humans being transformed into animals was a recurring theme in Celtic mythology, often as a form of punishment or curse. This reflected a belief in the power of magic to blur the lines between human and animal worlds.

The venomous nature of Twrch Trwyth's bristles also speaks to beliefs about the dangerous properties of certain animals. Just as some real animals were thought to be poisonous or have magical properties, so too was this mythical boar imbued with an extra level of danger.

The chase itself, covering vast distances and lasting for days, reflects beliefs about the supernatural stamina of mythical beasts. It also taps into ideas about the power of the landscape itself, with certain places being seen as more magical or powerful than others.

Connections to Other Myths

The story of Twrch Trwyth has fascinating connections to other mythologies. In Irish legend, we find a similar boar called Triath in the "Lebor Gabála Érenn" (The Book of Invasions). This connection suggests a shared Celtic heritage for these boar myths.

The theme of a great boar hunt also appears in other European mythologies. In Greek myth, we have the Calydonian Boar, a monstrous creature sent by Artemis to ravage the countryside. Like Twrch Trwyth, this boar was the subject of a great hunt involving many heroes.

In Norse mythology, the god Freyr owned a magical boar called Gullinbursti, while in Hindu myth, Vishnu took the form of a great boar called Varaha to battle demons. These parallels show how the image of the powerful, often magical boar resonated across many different cultures.

Welsh Landscape and Culture

The tale of Twrch Trwyth is deeply intertwined with the Welsh landscape. The chase takes Arthur and his men across recognisable regions of Wales, from the coastlines of Dyfed to the mountains of Snowdonia. This grounding in real geography helps to root the mythical tale in the physical world of medieval Wales.

The story also reflects aspects of Welsh culture and society.

The importance placed on hunting, the gathering of warriors for a common cause, and the leadership of a king like Arthur all mirror real aspects of Welsh life. Even the magical elements of the story, like transformation and mythical beasts, reflect the rich tradition of folklore and superstition that was an integral part of Welsh culture.

Today, the legend of Twrch Trwyth continues to be a part of Welsh cultural heritage. It's retold in books, featured in art, and even celebrated in traditional folk dances. The great boar hunt remains a powerful symbol of Welsh mythology, a tale that connects the modern Welsh people to their ancient past.

The story of Twrch Trwyth stands as a testament to the rich mythological tradition of Wales. It weaves together elements of magic, heroism, and the Welsh landscape into a tale that has captivated audiences for centuries. More than just an exciting adventure, it offers insights into medieval Welsh culture, beliefs, and the enduring power of myth to shape our understanding of the world around us.

Cyhyraeth

In the misty valleys and along the rugged coastlines of Wales, an eerie sound sometimes echoes through the night. It's a sound that chills the blood and sends shivers down the spine of even the bravest souls. This is the cry of the Cyhyraeth, a ghostly harbinger of death in Welsh folklore. For centuries, the people of Wales have whispered tales of this spectral entity, whose mournful wails foretell the end of life for those who hear it.

The Tale of the Cyhyraeth

The night was cold and damp in the small village near the River Tywi in eastern Dyfed. Owain, a local farmer, was walking home from the tavern when he heard it - a low, sorrowful moan that seemed to come from everywhere and nowhere at once. The sound was unlike anything he'd ever heard before, a mix of grief and warning that made his hair stand on end.

Owain quickened his pace, his heart pounding in his chest. The moan came again, this time slightly fainter. He broke into a run, desperate to reach the safety of his home. Just as he reached his front door, he heard it one last time - a barely audible whisper of despair that faded into the night.

Shaken, Owain burst into his house, startling his wife Megan. "What's wrong, cariad?" she asked, seeing the fear in his eyes. Owain recounted what he'd heard, and Megan's face paled.

"The Cyhyraeth," she whispered. "It's come for someone in the village."

For days, the villagers waited anxiously, wondering who the Cyhyraeth had marked for death. A week later, news came that old Mrs. Evans, who lived at the edge of the village, had passed away in her sleep.

But the Cyhyraeth's work wasn't done. A fortnight later, as storm clouds gathered over the Glamorganshire coast, fisherman Gareth Jones heard the same mournful cry while mending his nets. The sound seemed to come from the sea itself, growing fainter with each repetition. Gareth knew the legends and rushed to warn his fellow fishermen not to go out that night.

Most heeded his warning, but one boat, captained by Gareth's cousin Rhys, set sail despite the ominous signs. The next morning, pieces of Rhys's boat washed up on the shore. No bodies were ever found.

Historical Context and Origins

The legend of the Cyhyraeth is deeply rooted in Welsh folklore, particularly in the regions of eastern Dyfed and along the Glamorganshire coast. These areas, with their misty valleys and treacherous coastlines, provide the perfect backdrop for such a ghostly tale.

The Cyhyraeth belongs to a class of supernatural entities known as death omens, which are common in Celtic folklore. These beings, whether through sight or sound, warn of impending death. The concept reflects the deep-seated human fear of death and the unknown, as well as the desire to have some forewarning of life's end.

In Welsh culture, the Cyhyraeth serves a similar role to the banshee in Irish folklore. Both are spectral harbingers of death, often associated with specific families or areas. This similarity points to the shared Celtic heritage of these two cultures and the common threads that run through their mythology.

The legend of the Cyhyraeth likely evolved from earlier, pre-Christian beliefs. In many ancient cultures, death was seen not as an end, but as a transition to another state of being. Spirits or deities associated with death were often viewed as guides or heralds of this transition, rather than as purely malevolent entities.

Etymology and Symbolism

The exact etymology of 'Cyhyraeth' is uncertain, but it offers intriguing insights into the nature of this mythical being. One theory suggests that the first part of the word comes from "cyhyr," meaning "muscle" or "flesh." This could point to the physical nature of death that the Cyhyraeth foretells.

Another possibility is that it derives from "cyoer," related to "oer," meaning "cold." This interpretation aligns with the chilling nature of the Cyhyraeth's cry and the cold reality of death it represents.

The second part of the word might come from "aeth," meaning "pain" or "grief," or it could simply be the noun suffix "-aeth," similar to English "-ness" or "-ity." Either way, it emphasises the sorrowful nature of the entity.

The symbolism of the Cyhyraeth is rich and multi-layered. Its disembodied voice represents the intangible nature of death and the spirit world. The fact that it's heard rather than seen plays on the human fear of the unknown and unseen.

The threefold nature of its cry is significant in many cultures, where the number three is often seen as magical or sacred. In this case, it might represent the three stages of life: birth, life, and death. The diminishing volume of each cry could symbolise the fading of life force as death approaches.

Superstitions and Beliefs

The Cyhyraeth has given rise to various superstitions and beliefs among the Welsh people. Here are some of the most common:

- Hearing the Cyhyraeth's cry is considered an absolutely certain sign of impending death, either for the hearer or someone close to them.
- The Cyhyraeth is believed to be more active during stormy or misty weather, reflecting the treacherous nature of the Welsh coast.
- Some believe that the Cyhyraeth can be warded off by making the sign of the cross or reciting a prayer.
- In coastal areas, fishermen who hear the Cyhyraeth often refuse to go to sea, believing a shipwreck is imminent.
- The appearance of a corpse-light along with the Cyhyraeth's cry is seen as an especially potent death omen.

- Some traditions hold that the Cyhyraeth is more likely to appear to those with the "second sight" or other psychic abilities.

These beliefs reflect the deep-rooted fear and respect for death in Welsh culture, as well as the desire to find meaning and order in the often chaotic and unpredictable nature of mortality.

Connections to Other Myths

The Cyhyraeth shares similarities with death omens from other cultures, most notably the Irish banshee. Both are female spirits whose cries foretell death, often for specific families. This parallel demonstrates the shared Celtic heritage of Ireland and Wales.

The Cyhyraeth also bears some resemblance to the Greek sirens, whose haunting songs lured sailors to their doom. While the Cyhyraeth doesn't actively cause death, its association with shipwrecks along the Welsh coast creates a similar narrative of deadly voices from the sea.

In Norse mythology, the Valkyries were female figures who chose who would die in battle. While their role was more active than the Cyhyraeth's, they share the aspect of being female entities closely tied to death.

The concept of a spectral warning of death is also present in many Native American cultures. For example, the owl is often seen as a harbinger of death in various tribes, its cry serving a similar function to that of the Cyhyraeth.

Closely related to the Cyhyraeth in Welsh folklore is the Gwrach y Rhibyn, or Hag of the Mist. This frightening female spirit shares the Cyhyraeth's role as a death omen but takes a more visible and active form.

The Gwrach y Rhibyn is described as a hideously ugly woman with wild, unkempt hair, long black teeth, and wings like a bat. She's said to follow those marked for death, calling out to them at night or appearing at crossroads and streams.

Like the Cyhyraeth, the Gwrach y Rhibyn is associated with mist and water, often appearing in a rising fog. Some scholars speculate that she might have originally been a water deity or a form of the Welsh goddess Dôn, whose role was later demonised with the advent of Christianity.

The overlap between the Cyhyraeth and the Gwrach y Rhibyn highlights the complex nature of Welsh mythology, where different supernatural entities often share similar roles and characteristics. It also demonstrates how myths can evolve and blend over time, creating a rich tapestry of folklore.

The legend of the Cyhyraeth continues to captivate the imagination of people in Wales and beyond. It speaks to universal human fears about death and the unknown, while also reflecting the unique landscape and culture of Wales. From the misty valleys of Dyfed to the storm-tossed coasts of Glamorgan, the mournful cry of the Cyhyraeth remains a powerful symbol of the thin veil between life and death in Welsh folklore.

The Physicians of Myddfai

In the rolling hills of Carmarthenshire, Wales, a tale as old as the mountains themselves whispers through the valleys. It's a story of love, magic, and healing that has captivated the Welsh people for centuries. The legend of the Physicians of Myddfai is not just a fairy tale, but a cornerstone of Welsh medical folklore that blends the mystical with the practical.

The Tale of the Physicians of Myddfai

Long ago, in the shadow of the Black Mountain, there lived a young farmer near the shores of Llyn y Fan Fach. Each day, as he tended his cattle, he'd gaze upon the lake's mirror-like surface, hoping to catch a glimpse of the beautiful maidens said to dwell within its depths.

One fateful morning, as mist rolled off the water, a vision of loveliness emerged. A maiden with hair like spun gold and eyes as blue as the lake itself stood before him. The farmer's heart leapt, and he offered her his bread, but she smiled and slipped back into the water.

Undeterred, the farmer returned day after day, offering different breads until finally, the maiden accepted. As she took the bread, her father, a wizened old man, rose from the lake. He agreed to the maiden's marriage to the farmer, but with a stern warning: should the farmer strike his daughter three times without cause, she would return to the lake forever.

The couple lived happily for many years, blessed with three sons. But life has a way of testing even the strongest bonds. Thrice the farmer tapped his wife lightly - once when she laughed at a funeral, again when she cried at a wedding, and finally when she failed to bring his horse to a feast. Each time, she reminded him of her father's warning.

With the third tap, the maiden's eyes filled with sorrow. She called to her magical cattle and walked into the lake, never to return. Before she vanished, she left behind a gift for her sons - the knowledge of herbs and healing that would make them and their descendants famous throughout Wales.

These sons - Rhiwallon and his brothers - became the first of the Physicians of Myddfai. Their wisdom and skill in medicine passed down through generations, serving Welsh princes and common folk alike. For centuries, the Physicians of Myddfai practiced their art, their fame spreading far beyond the borders of Wales.

Historical Context and Origins

The legend of the Physicians of Myddfai is more than just a fanciful tale. It's rooted in the real medical practices of medieval Wales. The story first appeared in written form during the 13th century, coinciding with the time of Rhys Gryg, Prince of Deheubarth, who is said to have been served by Rhiwallon and his sons.

In those days, medicine was a blend of herbal lore, folk wisdom, and what we might now call superstition. The Physicians of Myddfai were renowned for their knowledge of herbs and their ability to cure ailments that baffled others. Their remedies, preserved in manuscripts like the Red Book of Hergest from the late 14th century, show a surprising sophistication for their time.

The legend's origins likely stem from a real family of healers who practiced in the Myddfai area. Over time, their skills became intertwined with local folklore, creating the magical origin story we know today. This blending of fact and fiction was common in medieval times, when the line between the natural and supernatural worlds was often blurred.

Etymology and Symbolism

The name 'Myddfai' itself is steeped in meaning. In Welsh, 'mydd' can mean 'soft' or 'yielding', while 'fai' might be related to 'mai', meaning 'field' or 'plain'. This could refer to the lush, fertile land around Myddfai, perfect for growing medicinal herbs.

The lake, Llyn y Fan Fach, symbolises the boundary between the mortal and fairy worlds. In Welsh folklore, lakes often serve as gateways to the Otherworld, home to magical beings. The maiden from the lake represents the supernatural source of the Physicians' knowledge, bridging the gap between human understanding and divine wisdom.

The three taps without cause in the story symbolise the fragility of agreements between mortals and fairy folk. They also serve as a moral lesson about the importance of treating others with respect and keeping one's word.

The tale of the Physicians of Myddfai is tied to several Welsh superstitions and beliefs:

- The power of liminal spaces: Lakes, like Llyn y Fan Fach, were seen as magical boundaries where otherworldly encounters were possible.
- Fairy brides: The belief that supernatural beings could marry mortals, often with strict conditions, was common in Welsh folklore.
- Inherited magical knowledge: The idea that special abilities or knowledge could be passed down through families was widespread.
- The healing power of nature: The Physicians' use of herbal remedies reflects the Welsh belief in the curative properties of plants and the natural world.

These beliefs shaped how people viewed health and healing in medieval Wales. Many would seek out the Physicians of Myddfai, believing their fairy-granted knowledge made them more effective than ordinary healers.

Connections to Other Myths

The story of the Physicians of Myddfai shares elements with other myths and legends from around the world:

- The tale of Melusine, a French water fairy who marries a mortal, has similar themes of conditional marriage between a supernatural being and a human.

- The Irish legend of Oisín and Niamh has parallels, with a mortal man entering a magical realm and being bound by certain rules.
- The Greek myth of Orpheus and Eurydice also deals with the consequences of breaking conditions set by supernatural beings.

In Wales itself, the story connects to other lake-maiden legends, such as the Lady of Llyn y Fan Fach, which likely influenced or was influenced by the Physicians' tale.

The Legacy of the Myddfai Physicians

The impact of the Physicians of Myddfai on Welsh culture cannot be overstated. Their legend has inspired countless retellings, from medieval manuscripts to modern literature. The herbal remedies attributed to them continued to be used well into the 18th century, with some still finding use in folk medicine today.

The story also highlights the importance of the natural world in Welsh culture. The Physicians' knowledge of herbs and their connection to the land reflect a deep respect for nature that remains a part of Welsh identity.

Today, the village of Myddfai continues to honour its legendary healers through The Physicians of Myddfai Society, established in 2014. The society aims to promote and raise the profile of this historic medical tradition through cultural, educational, and scientific activities. The Myddfai Community Hall and Visitors Centre, opened in 2011, serves as a hub for the society's annual conferences and other events. Here, visitors can explore the area's rich medical heritage, including the legend of Llyn y Fan Fach and the tradition of healing waters, which are central themes in the society's programming and local initiatives.

The tale of the Physicians of Myddfai is more than just a story - it's a window into the beliefs, practices, and values of medieval Wales. It reminds us of a time when magic and medicine were intertwined, and when the wisdom of the natural world was held in the highest regard. As long as people continue to be fascinated by the intersection of folklore and healing, the legend of the Physicians of Myddfai will live on, a testament to Wales's rich cultural heritage.

The story of the Physicians of Myddfai continues to captivate us, bridging the gap between myth and reality. It speaks to our enduring fascination with the healing arts and our connection to the natural world. In the mist-shrouded valleys of Wales, the legacy of these legendary healers lives on, reminding us of the magic that can be found in the land and in the wisdom passed down through generations.

Twm Siôn Cati

In the rolling hills of mid-Wales, where mist clings to the valleys and ancient forests whisper tales of old, there lived a man whose name would become legendary. Twm Siôn Cati, the Welsh trickster and folk hero, has captured the imagination of generations with his cunning exploits and clever schemes. His story is woven into the fabric of Welsh folklore, a testament to the enduring appeal of a quick-witted underdog who outsmarted both the law and the lawless.

The Tale of Twm Siôn Cati

In the bustling market town of Tregaron, nestled in the heart of Ceredigion, a boy was born to Cati Jones and Siôn ap Dafydd ap Madog around the year 1530. This lad, christened Thomas, would grow to become the infamous Twm Siôn Cati, a name that would echo through the ages in Welsh folklore.

As a young man, Twm found himself in a world turned upside down. Queen Mary I sat on the English throne, and her fierce determination to return England to Catholicism sent tremors through the land. For Twm, a Protestant of humble birth, these were dangerous times indeed. With few options available to him, he turned to a life of roguery and mischief.

One tale speaks of Twm's clever ruse to steal a farmer's horse and money. Disguised as a beggar, he approached the farmer on the road, spinning a tale of woe. The kind-hearted farmer, moved by Twm's plight, dismounted to offer him a few coins. Quick as a flash, Twm leapt onto the horse and galloped away, leaving the bewildered farmer standing in the dust.

Another story tells of Twm's ingenuity in helping a friend steal a pitcher. Together, they visited a merchant's shop where Twm enacted a clever ruse. He began by criticising the merchant's wares - Twm claimed one of the pitchers had a hole. When the merchant denied this, Twm challenged him to put his hand inside the pitcher to verify. As the merchant did so, Twm posed a logical trap: "If there's no hole, how did you put your hand inside?" This witty exchange so occupied the merchant that Twm's friend was able to depart unnoticed with his chosen pitcher, highlighting Twm's quick thinking and verbal dexterity.

But Twm's tricks weren't limited to helping himself and his friends. He often used his wit to outwit other criminals, particularly highwaymen who preyed on travellers. In one such encounter, Twm fooled a group of bandits by pretending to hide a great treasure in his pack-saddle. The thieves, overcome with greed, stole the saddle and fled, only to find it stuffed with worthless straw.

As the law closed in on Twm, he fled to Geneva in 1557. But Wales called to him, and he returned in 1559, pardoned by the newly crowned Queen Elizabeth I. This marked a turning point in Twm's life. He set aside his roguish ways and, through a fortunate marriage to a wealthy widow, transformed himself into a respectable member of society. The once-notorious outlaw became a magistrate and even served as mayor, using his keen understanding of the criminal mind to uphold the very laws he had once flouted.

Yet even as a man of standing, Twm's wit never left him. It's said that he would often disguise himself as a beggar to test the charity of his neighbours, always ready with a lesson for those who turned him away empty-handed.

As Twm grew old, he became a local legend. People would gather in taverns and around firesides to share tales of his exploits, each story growing taller with each retelling. And so, Twm Siôn Cati passed into legend, a Welsh Robin Hood whose quick wit and clever tricks continue to captivate audiences to this day.

Historical Context and Origins

The story of Twm Siôn Cati is deeply rooted in the turbulent history of 16th century Wales. This was a time of great religious and social upheaval, as the Protestant Reformation swept across Europe and reached the shores of Britain. The reign of Mary I (1553-1558) saw a violent attempt to restore Catholicism, which put Protestants like Twm in a precarious position.

The real Thomas Jones, believed to be the inspiration for Twm Siôn Cati, was born around 1530 near Tregaron. His life spanned a period of significant change in Wales, as the country grappled with its place within the newly formed Kingdom of England and Wales. The Act of Union in 1536 had brought Wales more firmly under English control, leading to social and economic shifts that often disadvantaged the Welsh people.

In this context, Twm's story of a clever underdog outwitting authority figures resonated strongly with the Welsh population. His exploits, whether real or embellished, became a form of cultural resistance against English dominance and a celebration of Welsh ingenuity.

It's important to remember that the stories of Twm Siôn Cati we know today are likely a blend of fact and fiction. The historical Thomas Jones did indeed receive a pardon in 1559, wrote poetry, and married a widow who improved his social standing. However, many of the more colourful tales associated with Twm probably amalgamate stories of several individuals sharing the name Thomas Jones, a common name in Wales.

The first written accounts of Twm's exploits appeared much later, with the earliest known pamphlet published in 1763. This was followed by books in the 1820s and an influential novel by T.J. Llewelyn Prichard in 1828. These works helped to cement Twm's place in Welsh folklore and spread his fame beyond the borders of Ceredigion.

Etymology and Symbolism

The name Twm Siôn Cati itself is a reflection of Welsh naming customs of the time. 'Twm' is a diminutive form of 'Thomas', while 'Siôn' (John) was his father's name, and 'Cati' (Catherine) his mother's. This naming pattern, using the father's and sometimes the mother's name, was common in Wales and served to distinguish individuals in communities where many shared the same first name.

Symbolically, Twm represents the archetypal trickster figure found in many cultures' mythologies. Like Loki in Norse myths or Anansi in West African folklore, Twm uses his wit and cunning to overcome challenges and often subvert social norms. His ability to outsmart both criminals and law-abiding citizens alike symbolises the power of intelligence over brute force or social status.

The transformation of Twm from outlaw to respectable citizen also carries symbolic weight. It reflects the Welsh ideal of 'gwerin' - the common people who, through education and hard work, could rise to positions of respect and authority. Twm's journey from rogue to magistrate embodies this aspiration for social mobility.

Superstitions and Beliefs

While not associated with specific superstitions, the tales of Twm Siôn Cati reflect certain beliefs and values of Welsh society at the time. His clever tricks often rewarded kindness and punished greed or cruelty, reinforcing moral lessons through storytelling.

The cave on Dinas Hill, said to have been Twm's hideout, became a site of local folklore. People believed that touching the cave walls could bring good luck or grant a portion of Twm's legendary cleverness.

There was also a belief that Twm had the ability to shape-shift or become invisible, a common attribute of trickster figures in folklore. These supernatural elements added to his mystique and made his escapes from justice seem more plausible to storytellers and listeners alike.

Connections to Other Myths

Twm Siôn Cati shares many characteristics with trickster figures from other cultures. His clever schemes and ability to outwit authority figures are reminiscent of Reynard the Fox in European folklore or the Coyote in Native American tales.

Perhaps the most obvious parallel is with Robin Hood, the English outlaw hero. Like Robin, Twm is portrayed as a clever rogue who steals from the rich, though Twm's motivations are more self-serving than Robin's legendary generosity to the poor. Both figures, however, represent a form of social banditry that appealed to common people living under oppressive systems.

In Irish folklore, there's a similar figure named Seán na Sagart (John of the Priests), a priest-hunter turned priest-protector whose story shares themes of redemption and cleverness with Twm's tale.

The motif of the trickster who eventually gains respectability is also found in the story of Odysseus in Greek mythology, who uses his wit to overcome challenges and eventually reclaims his place as king of Ithaca.

Twm Siôn Cati in Welsh Culture

Twm's legacy in Welsh culture extends far beyond the original tales. His story has been adapted into various forms of media, including literature, theatre, and television. The 1978 TV series "Hawkmoor" portrayed Twm as a Welsh Robin Hood figure, introducing his legend to a new generation.

In Tregaron, Twm's supposed hometown, his memory is celebrated with an annual Twm Siôn Cati Day. The event features re-enactments of his exploits and celebrates Welsh culture and history. In 2009, the community marked the 400th anniversary of his death with special commemorative events.

Twm has also found his way into children's literature, with numerous books retelling his adventures for young readers. These modern adaptations often emphasise his cleverness and the moral lessons in his tales, continuing the oral tradition of using stories to entertain and educate.

The cave on Dinas Hill, known as 'Twm Siôn Cati's Cave', has become a minor tourist attraction. Visitors can hike to the cave and imagine the legendary outlaw planning his next caper in this rugged hideout.

The enduring popularity of Twm Siôn Cati speaks to the universal appeal of the clever underdog who uses wit to overcome adversity. His tales, born in the mist-shrouded hills of mid-Wales, have become a cherished part of Welsh cultural identity. They remind us of a time when quick thinking and a silver tongue could turn the tables on the powerful, and when a rogue could become a hero in the eyes of the people. As long as there are storytellers in Wales, the legend of Twm Siôn Cati will continue to enthral and inspire, a beloved thread in the rich tapestry of Welsh folklore.

Gelert

In the misty hills of Gwynedd, North-West Wales, there's a village called Beddgelert. Its name, meaning "Gelert's Grave," holds a story that has touched hearts for generations. This is the tale of Gelert, a brave wolfhound whose unwavering loyalty led to a tragic misunderstanding.

The Tale of Gelert

Long ago, in the time of Llywelyn the Great, a prince of Gwynedd, there lived a magnificent wolfhound named Gelert. Llywelyn had received Gelert as a gift, and the dog quickly became his most faithful companion. Gelert was known throughout the land for his strength, courage, and unwavering loyalty to his master.

One crisp autumn morning, Llywelyn prepared for a hunt in the nearby forests. As he readied his horse and gathered his weapons, he noticed Gelert was nowhere to be found. This was unusual, as the loyal hound always accompanied him on hunts. Puzzled but not overly concerned, Llywelyn set off without his canine friend.

The hunt was long and tiring. As the sun began to set, Llywelyn returned to his home, eager to see his infant son and his beloved Gelert. As he approached, he heard the excited barks of his dog. Smiling, Llywelyn quickened his pace, looking forward to the warm welcome he always received.

But as he entered his home, a chilling sight met his eyes. The nursery was in disarray, the cradle overturned, and there was no sign of his baby. Gelert bounded up to him, tail wagging, but to Llywelyn's horror, the dog's muzzle was smeared with blood.

In that terrible moment, Llywelyn's mind raced to the worst conclusion. Consumed by grief and rage, he drew his sword and struck down Gelert where he stood. The faithful hound let out a single, heart-rending yelp as he fell.

As Gelert's cry echoed through the room, Llywelyn heard another sound - the cry of his baby. Frantically, he searched the nursery and found his son, alive and unharmed, hidden beneath the overturned cradle. And there, lying dead beside the cradle, was a massive wolf.

The truth dawned on Llywelyn with devastating clarity. Gelert had not harmed the child; he had protected him. The brave dog had fought and killed the wolf that had threatened the baby's life.

Overcome with remorse, Llywelyn cradled Gelert's body, his tears falling on the faithful hound's fur. He had killed his most loyal friend, the true protector of his family. From that day forward, it's said that Llywelyn never smiled again.

To honour Gelert's memory and loyalty, Llywelyn buried him with great ceremony. He erected a tomb for the faithful hound, and the place became known as Beddgelert - "Gelert's Grave."

The story of Gelert is a powerful tale that has captured imaginations for centuries. However, like many legends, its historical accuracy is questionable. Historians generally agree that Gelert, as portrayed in the story, likely never existed.

The village of Beddgelert, despite its name, probably wasn't named after the legendary dog. Instead, it's believed the name comes from an early Christian saint named Celert or Kilart, who may have founded a church in the area.

The story as we know it today seems to have emerged in the late 18th century. It was likely popularised by David Pritchard, a local innkeeper who saw an opportunity to attract tourists to the area. Pritchard is believed to have created the raised mound known as "Gelert's Grave" and may have been instrumental in spreading the tale.

Despite its relatively recent origins, the legend of Gelert taps into much older storytelling traditions. It's an example of what folklorists call the "Faithful Hound" motif, a type of story found in many cultures around the world.

The basic plot - a loyal animal protector being mistakenly killed by its master - appears in folklore from India, Malaysia, and various European countries.

In Wales, the story found fertile ground. The Welsh have a long tradition of folklore and legend, and the tale of Gelert fit well with existing stories of loyal animals and tragic misunderstandings. It also aligned with the historical importance of dogs in Welsh culture, particularly large breeds like wolfhounds that were used for hunting and protection.

The setting of the story in the time of Llywelyn the Great adds another layer of historical intrigue. Llywelyn, who ruled in the early 13th century, was a significant figure in Welsh history. He was known for his military prowess and political acumen, successfully resisting English dominance and uniting much of Wales under his rule. By associating the legend with such a renowned historical figure, the story gained additional gravitas and appeal.

Etymology and Symbolism

The name "Gelert" itself is intriguing. While its exact origin is unclear, it may be related to the Welsh word "celer," meaning "faithful" or "loyal." This etymology would be fitting given the central theme of the story.

The symbolism in the tale is rich and multi-layered. Gelert, the faithful hound, represents unwavering loyalty and the bond between humans and animals. His actions in defending the baby from the wolf symbolise the protective instinct and the nobility of self-sacrifice.

The wolf, on the other hand, embodies the wild and dangerous aspects of nature. In many European folktales, wolves are portrayed as threats to domesticated life, often targeting the young and vulnerable. The conflict between Gelert and the wolf can be seen as a metaphor for the struggle between civilisation and wilderness.

Llywelyn's hasty judgement and tragic mistake serve as a cautionary tale about the dangers of acting on assumptions without full knowledge. His remorse and the establishment of Gelert's grave symbolise the human capacity for recognising error and seeking redemption.

The overturned cradle is another potent symbol. It represents the fragility of life and the constant threats faced by the young and helpless. That the baby survives hidden beneath it could be seen as a message of hope and resilience in the face of danger.

Superstitions and Beliefs

While the story of Gelert isn't directly tied to specific superstitions, it does reflect and reinforce certain beliefs that were common in medieval Wales and beyond.

One such belief was the idea that dogs, especially large breeds like wolfhounds, had a special protective instinct towards children. This notion wasn't unique to Wales; similar beliefs existed across Europe and can be found in various folktales and legends.

The story also plays into superstitions about wolves. In many rural communities, wolves were seen as embodiments of the dangerous wild, threats to livestock and children alike. The fear of wolves was deeply ingrained in folk belief, often extending beyond the actual threat they posed.

There's also an element of the supernatural in some tellings of the story. Some versions suggest that Llywelyn was cursed never to smile again as punishment for his hasty action. This reflects a common belief in divine or supernatural justice, where wrongdoings, even if unintentional, could result in lasting consequences.

The creation of Gelert's grave and the naming of Beddgelert after the loyal hound reflect another common practice: the establishment of memorial sites for legendary or heroic figures. Such sites often became focal points for local identity and, in some cases, objects of pilgrimage or tourism.

Connections to Other Myths

The tale of Gelert shares similarities with stories from various cultures around the world. One of the closest parallels is the Indian folktale of the mongoose and the brahmin, where a mongoose protects a child from a snake but is killed by the returning father who misinterprets the blood on its mouth.

In Alpine folklore, there's a similar story about a faithful dog named Barry who saves a child from an avalanche but is mistakenly shot by a rescue party. The Malaysian folktale of Si Kikir tells of a dog who saves his master's baby from a snake but is killed in a misunderstanding.

Even ancient Egypt had a version of this story, featuring the god Anubis as the faithful protector. In this tale, Anubis guards the body of Osiris but is initially suspected of harming him.

These widespread occurrences of the "Faithful Hound" motif suggest a universal human concern with themes of loyalty, misunderstanding, and tragic irony. The story seems to resonate across cultures, perhaps because it touches on fundamental aspects of the human-animal bond and the potential for tragic misunderstandings.

The legend of Gelert is deeply rooted in the Welsh landscape. Snowdonia, where Beddgelert is located, is a region of stunning natural beauty, with rugged mountains, deep valleys, and ancient forests. This dramatic scenery provides a fitting backdrop for such a powerful tale.

In Welsh culture, dogs, especially large breeds like wolfhounds, have long held a special place. They were valued for their hunting skills, their protective instincts, and their loyalty. The Welsh laws of Hywel Dda, codified in the 10th century, included specific provisions about the value and treatment of dogs, indicating their importance in society.

The story also reflects the historical importance of wolves in Wales. While wolves were extinct in Wales by the 16th century, they remained a powerful symbol in folklore and legend. The conflict between the domesticated dog and the wild wolf in the story of Gelert echoes the broader tension between civilisation and wilderness that characterised much of Welsh history.

The legend of Gelert, with its themes of loyalty, tragedy, and redemption, continues to captivate people today. While historians may debate its historical accuracy, the emotional truth of the story resonates deeply. It speaks to the enduring bond between humans and dogs, the potential for tragic misunderstandings, and the importance of trust and careful judgement.

The tale has become an integral part of Welsh folklore, drawing visitors to Beddgelert and keeping alive a tradition of storytelling that stretches back centuries. Whether seen as a historical event, a moral fable, or simply a touching story, the legend of Gelert remains a powerful testament to the complex relationships between humans, animals, and the wild world around us.

Ceridwen

In the misty valleys and rolling hills of Wales, where ancient tales whisper on the wind, there lived a powerful enchantress named Ceridwen. Her story, woven into the fabric of Welsh mythology, speaks of magic, transformation, and the pursuit of knowledge. This legend has captivated the imagination of the Welsh people for centuries, offering a glimpse into the rich tapestry of Celtic lore.

The Tale of Ceridwen

Long ago, in a grand house near the shores of Bala Lake in North Wales, lived Ceridwen with her husband Tegid Foel and their two children. Their son, Morfran, was cursed with terrible ugliness, while their daughter, Creirwy, was blessed with extraordinary beauty. Ceridwen, a skilled sorceress, was determined to help her unfortunate son.

In her magical cauldron, Ceridwen began to brew a potion of wisdom and poetic inspiration, known as Awen. This enchanted brew would take a year and a day to complete, requiring constant stirring. Ceridwen enlisted a young lad named Gwion Bach to tend the cauldron.

Day after day, Gwion stirred the bubbling mixture. As the final moments approached, three drops of the potion splashed onto Gwion's thumb. Instinctively, he licked the burning liquid from his skin. In that instant, all the wisdom and knowledge meant for Morfran flooded into Gwion's mind.

Ceridwen, realising what had happened, flew into a rage. Gwion, now gifted with foresight, fled in terror. What followed was a wild chase across the Welsh countryside, with both Ceridwen and Gwion shape-shifting into various creatures.

Gwion turned himself into a hare, bounding across fields, but Ceridwen became a greyhound, swiftly gaining ground. He leapt into a river, becoming a fish, but she transformed into an otter, cutting through the water with ease. Gwion took to the sky as a bird, but Ceridwen pursued as a hawk, her keen eyes fixed on her prey.

In a final desperate act, Gwion became a single grain of wheat, hiding among a pile of grain on a threshing floor. But Ceridwen, ever clever, turned herself into a black hen. She pecked at the grain until she found and swallowed Gwion.

Nine months later, Ceridwen gave birth to a beautiful baby boy. Despite her initial anger, she couldn't bring herself to harm the child. Instead, she placed him in a leather bag and cast him into the sea. The waves carried the infant to the fishing weir of Gwyddno Garanhir, where he was discovered by the prince Elphin. The boy grew to become Taliesin, the greatest bard in all of Britain.

Historical Context and Origins

The tale of Ceridwen is deeply rooted in Welsh oral tradition, with its earliest written version appearing in a 16th-century manuscript. However, the story's origins likely stretch back much further, possibly to the 9th century. This legend reflects the Welsh people's reverence for poetry and the bardic tradition, as well as their belief in the transformative power of knowledge.

Ceridwen's character has evolved over time. In early Welsh poetry, she was associated with the cauldron of poetic inspiration. By the 12th century, poets began to portray her as a goddess of poetry. This transformation shows how myths can change and grow with the cultural needs of a society.

The setting of the story near Bala Lake (Llyn Tegid) in North Wales grounds the myth in the Welsh landscape. This connection to place is a common feature in Celtic mythology, where the natural world often plays a significant role. The lake itself has become associated with magic and mystery in local folklore, partly due to its connection with Ceridwen's legend.

The chase sequence in the story, where Ceridwen and Gwion transform into various animals, showcases the shape-shifting motif common in Celtic mythology. This element of the tale likely has roots in ancient beliefs about the connection between humans and nature, as well as the fluid nature of reality in a world filled with magic.

Etymology and Symbolism

The name Ceridwen itself has been the subject of much scholarly debate. It appears in various forms in early manuscripts, including 'Kyrridven,' 'Kyrrytuen,' and 'Cerituen.' The ending '-wen' or '-ven' comes from the old Welsh word for 'woman.' Some scholars have suggested that the name might mean "crooked woman" or "woman to be believed in," though its exact meaning remains uncertain.

Ceridwen's cauldron is a powerful symbol in the story. Cauldrons feature prominently in Celtic mythology, often associated with abundance, rebirth, and transformation. In this tale, the cauldron represents the vessel of knowledge and inspiration, echoing the importance of poetic skill in Welsh culture.

The three drops of the potion that grant wisdom to Gwion reflect a common motif in Celtic stories, where magical powers often come in threes. This could be linked to the broader Indo-European concept of the sacred number three, which appears in many mythologies and religions.

Superstitions and Beliefs

The legend of Ceridwen has given rise to various superstitions and beliefs in Welsh folklore. Some people believed that drinking water from Bala Lake could impart wisdom or poetic inspiration, echoing the magical properties of Ceridwen's cauldron.

In some traditions, Ceridwen became associated with the moon and its cycles, possibly due to the nine-month gestation period mentioned in the story. This led to practices where people would appeal to Ceridwen for help with fertility or childbirth.

The concept of Awen, the poetic inspiration in Ceridwen's cauldron, has remained significant in Welsh culture. Some modern-day poets and storytellers still invoke Ceridwen or the spirit of Awen when seeking inspiration for their work.

Ceridwen's tale shares similarities with other myths from Celtic and broader European folklore. The chase sequence, where characters transform into animals, is reminiscent of the Irish legend of Tuan mac Cairill, who lived through various animal incarnations.

The theme of accidentally gaining wisdom through tasting a magical substance appears in the Irish tale of Finn MacCool and the Salmon of Knowledge. In this story, Finn gains wisdom by sucking his thumb after it is burned while cooking the magical salmon.

The motif of a child cast adrift in a container and later becoming a great person is found in many cultures. It echoes the biblical story of Moses, as well as the Roman legend of Romulus and Remus.

Ceridwen in Modern Paganism

In recent times, Ceridwen has found a new role in modern pagan and neo-druid traditions. She is often venerated as a goddess of rebirth, transformation, and inspiration. Her cauldron has become a symbol of the womb and the cyclical nature of life, death, and rebirth.

Some modern practitioners use meditation or visualisation techniques to connect with Ceridwen's energy, seeking inspiration or guidance for personal transformation. Others incorporate symbols associated with her, such as cauldrons or moon imagery, into their spiritual practices.

This modern interpretation of Ceridwen shows how ancient myths can find new relevance and meaning in contemporary spiritual movements, while still maintaining a connection to their Welsh roots.

The legend of Ceridwen continues to captivate and inspire, offering insights into the values and beliefs of medieval Welsh society while resonating with modern audiences. Her story speaks to universal themes of the pursuit of knowledge, the power of transformation, and the enduring nature of wisdom. As long as people gather to share tales in the shadow of Welsh mountains or by the shores of misty lakes, Ceridwen's magic will continue to enchant and transform.

King Arthur

In the mists of ancient Wales, where rolling hills meet rugged coastlines, a tale of heroism, magic, and destiny was born. The story of King Arthur, a figure who has captivated imaginations for centuries, is deeply rooted in Welsh soil and folklore. This legendary king, with his fabled sword Excalibur and his noble Knights of the Round Table, has become a symbol of chivalry, justice, and the enduring spirit of the Welsh people.

The Tale of King Arthur

In a time of great turmoil, when Britain was beset by invaders and the old ways were fading, a boy named Arthur was born to King Uther Pendragon and Igraine of Cornwall. To protect the child from his enemies, the wizard Merlin spirited Arthur away to be raised in secret by Sir Ector, a loyal knight.

As Arthur grew, Britain fell into chaos. The land cried out for a true king to unite the people. Merlin, guided by ancient prophecy, placed a magical sword in a stone, declaring that only the rightful king could pull it free.

Many tried and failed to extract the sword, but young Arthur, unaware of his royal lineage, effortlessly drew it forth. With this act, he was revealed as the true heir to the throne of Britain.

As king, Arthur established his court at Camelot and gathered the bravest and most noble knights in the land. They sat at the Round Table, where all were considered equals. Among these knights were Sir Lancelot, Sir Gawain, and Sir Percival.

Arthur's reign brought peace and prosperity to the land. He wielded Excalibur, a magical sword given to him by the Lady of the Lake, and with it, he vanquished Britain's foes and upheld justice throughout the realm.

But even the greatest of kings are not immune to tragedy. Arthur's half-sister, Morgan le Fay, plotted against him. His most trusted knight, Lancelot, fell in love with Queen Guinevere, Arthur's wife. This betrayal tore the kingdom apart.

In the end, Arthur faced his greatest challenge in Mordred, his own son born of an unwitting union with his half-sister Morgause. In a final, devastating battle at Camlann, Arthur and Mordred mortally wounded each other.

As Arthur lay dying, he commanded Sir Bedivere to return Excalibur to the Lady of the Lake. Then, the king was borne away to the mystical isle of Avalon. It is said that Arthur sleeps there still, ready to return in Britain's hour of greatest need – the Once and Future King.

Historical Context and Origins

The tale of King Arthur is a complex tapestry woven from history, myth, and literary invention and with links to all four corners of the British Isles. While the historical existence of Arthur remains a subject of debate, his legend is deeply intertwined with the history and culture of Wales.

The roots of the Arthurian legend can be traced back to the

tumultuous period following the withdrawal of Roman forces from Britain in the 5th century. This era, known as the Dark Ages, saw the native Britons (ancestors of the Welsh) struggling against invading Anglo-Saxons.

Early Welsh texts, such as the "Annales Cambriae" and the "Historia Brittonum," mention Arthur as a warrior who led the Britons in battles against the Saxon invaders. These accounts, while sparse, suggest that stories of a heroic leader named Arthur were circulating in Wales by the 9th century.

The character of Arthur as we know him today began to take shape in the 12th century with Geoffrey of Monmouth's "Historia Regum Britanniae" (History of the Kings of Britain). Geoffrey, a Welsh cleric, drew on earlier Welsh traditions and his own imagination to create a grand narrative of British history, with Arthur at its centre.

Geoffrey's work was hugely influential, sparking a wave of Arthurian literature across Europe. French writers, particularly Chrétien de Troyes, added romantic elements and new characters like Lancelot and the Holy Grail. These continental versions often overshadowed the Welsh origins of the legend.

However, Arthur remained an important figure in Welsh culture. Medieval Welsh texts like the "Mabinogion" contain stories that present Arthur in a more Celtic light, as a supernatural hero associated with the Otherworld.

The Arthurian legend evolved over time, reflecting changing social and cultural values. In the Victorian era, writers like

Alfred Tennyson reimagined Arthur as the perfect gentleman, embodying ideals of chivalry and moral virtue.

Today, historians and archaeologists continue to search for evidence of a historical Arthur. While some associate him with Roman-British leaders or Welsh chieftains of the post-Roman period, no conclusive proof of his existence has been found.

Etymology and Symbolism

The name "Arthur" itself has been the subject of much scholarly debate. One popular theory suggests it derives from the Roman name Artorius. Others propose Celtic origins, possibly related to the Welsh word "arth," meaning "bear," symbolising strength and leadership.

Excalibur, Arthur's magical sword, is a potent symbol of rightful kingship and divine favour. Its name may come from the Welsh "Caledfwlch," meaning "hard cleft" or "hard lightning."

The Round Table represents equality and unity, core values of Arthur's reign. Its circular shape ensures that no knight can claim precedence over another, embodying the ideal of a just and harmonious society.

The Holy Grail, introduced in later versions of the legend, symbolises spiritual perfection and the quest for divine grace. It adds a mystical and Christian dimension to the originally pagan Celtic tale.

Superstitions and Beliefs

Arthurian legend is rich with magical and supernatural elements that reflect ancient Welsh beliefs. Merlin, the powerful wizard, embodies the Welsh tradition of prophets and seers. His ability to shapeshift and command magical forces echoes the powers attributed to druids in Celtic lore.

The Lady of the Lake, who gives Arthur Excalibur, represents the Celtic belief in powerful female deities associated with water. Lakes and other bodies of water were often seen as gateways to the Otherworld in Welsh mythology.

The idea that Arthur sleeps in Avalon, ready to return in Britain's hour of need, reflects a common Celtic belief in the "king under the mountain" motif. This concept of a sleeping hero who will awaken to save his people is found in many Welsh legends.

Connections to Other Myths

The Arthurian legend shares themes and motifs with myths from around the world. The concept of the rightful king proven by drawing a sword from a stone is reminiscent of Thor's hammer in Norse mythology, which only the worthy could lift.

Arthur's magical sword, Excalibur, has parallels in many cultures, such as Kusanagi in Japanese mythology or Durandal in the French epic "The Song of Roland."

The tragic love triangle of Arthur, Guinevere, and Lancelot echoes the Irish legend of Deirdre, Naoise, and King Conchobar, highlighting the universal theme of love versus duty.

The landscape of Wales is dotted with sites associated with Arthur. Cadbury Castle in Somerset, just over the border from Wales, has been identified by some as a possible location for Camelot. In Snowdonia, the lake Llyn Llydaw is sometimes named as the home of the Lady of the Lake.

The hill fort of Dinas Emrys in Gwynedd is linked to the legend of Merlin and the red and white dragons, a story central to Welsh national identity. These physical connections to the landscape help keep the Arthurian legend alive in the hearts and imaginations of the Welsh people.

King Arthur's legend, born from the misty hills and ancient traditions of Wales, has grown to become a cornerstone of Western literature and popular culture. While the historical Arthur may remain elusive, his story continues to inspire and captivate audiences worldwide. In Wales, Arthur is more than just a legendary king – he is a symbol of national identity, a reminder of the country's rich cultural heritage, and a testament to the enduring power of myth. As long as people dream of heroism, justice, and the triumph of good over evil, the tale of King Arthur will continue to be told, retold, and reimagined, keeping the spirit of ancient Wales alive in the modern world.

The Lady of the Lake

In the misty hills of Wales, where ancient forests hide secrets as old as time itself, the tale of the Lady of the Lake has been whispered for generations. This mysterious figure, part of the rich tapestry of Arthurian legend, has captivated imaginations for centuries. Her story is as changeable as the waters she's said to inhabit, with many versions painting her as a powerful enchantress, a guardian of magical artefacts, and a key player in the fate of King Arthur and his knights.

The Tale of the Lady of the Lake

Picture a serene lake nestled in the Welsh countryside, its surface as smooth as glass, reflecting the green hills and cloudy skies above. It's here, in these tranquil waters, that the Lady of the Lake makes her home.

As the story goes, young Arthur, guided by the wizard Merlin, approached the lake's edge. The air was thick with anticipation, and Arthur's heart raced as he gazed out over the still waters. Suddenly, the lake's surface began to ripple, and from its depths emerged a slender arm, clothed in shimmering white samite. In its grasp was a magnificent sword - Excalibur.

The Lady of the Lake, her face hidden beneath the water's surface, offered the sword to Arthur. "Take this sword, young king," her voice echoed across the water, "for it is Excalibur, and with it, you shall rule justly and bring peace to the land."

Arthur reached out and took the sword, marvelling at its perfect balance and gleaming blade. As he raised it above his head, sunlight glinted off its surface, and he felt the weight of destiny settle upon his shoulders.

But the Lady of the Lake's role in Arthurian legend doesn't end there. In some tellings, she's also known as Nimue, the enchantress who became Merlin's apprentice. Merlin, besotted with her beauty and keen mind, taught her all his magical secrets. But Nimue, wary of the wizard's advances and desiring her freedom, used these very same secrets against him.

One day, as they walked through a forest, Nimue convinced Merlin to show her a powerful spell. As he demonstrated, she quickly turned the magic against him, trapping him forever in a tree or beneath a great stone. Some say she did this out of malice, others out of self-defence, but regardless, it marked the end of Merlin's influence over Arthur's court.

The Lady of the Lake's influence extended beyond these pivotal moments. She's often credited with raising Sir Lancelot after the death of his father, King Ban. She bestowed upon him magical gifts and guided him towards becoming one of Arthur's greatest knights.

As Arthur's reign neared its end, mortally wounded after the battle of Camlann, it was the Lady of the Lake who came to his aid. She appeared in a boat, ready to ferry the dying king to the mystical isle of Avalon, where he could heal and, perhaps one day, return.

The Lady of the Lake, like many figures in Arthurian legend, has roots that stretch back into the mists of time, intertwining with Celtic mythology and medieval romance. Her character evolved over centuries, with different storytellers adding layers to her legend.

In Welsh mythology, there are numerous tales of magical women associated with lakes. The goddess Ceridwen, for instance, was said to live near Lake Bala in North Wales. These early myths likely influenced the later development of the Lady of the Lake character.

The first written mentions of a Lady of the Lake appear in French romances of the 13th century. In these early stories, she's often portrayed as a powerful fairy or enchantress, sometimes benevolent, sometimes dangerous. The name Nimue, along with variants like Viviane and Ninianne, began to be associated with her around this time.

It's worth noting that there isn't just one Lady of the Lake in these stories. Different texts present multiple enchantresses with this title, each playing various roles in the Arthurian saga. This multiplicity reflects the complex and often contradictory nature of medieval storytelling, where different traditions and local legends were woven together over time.

The Lady of the Lake's connection to Excalibur became particularly prominent in later medieval works. In Sir Thomas Malory's "Le Morte d'Arthur," published in 1485, she plays a crucial role in providing Arthur with his legendary sword. This version of the story has become one of the most enduring, influencing countless retellings in the centuries since.

Etymology and Symbolism

The names associated with the Lady of the Lake are rich with meaning and possible interpretations. 'Nimue' is thought by some scholars to be related to 'Mneme', the Greek word for 'memory'. This could symbolise her role as a keeper of ancient wisdom and magic.

'Viviane', another common name for her, has been linked to the Celtic word 'Co-Viana', meaning 'fair' or 'blessed'. Some theories connect it to the Welsh word 'chwyfleian', which means 'to move in a fluid, undulating motion' - quite fitting for a lady of the waters!

The Lady of the Lake herself is often seen as a symbol of the otherworldly and magical aspects of nature. Her domain, the lake, represents the boundary between the mortal world and the supernatural realm. Water, with its reflective surface and hidden depths, has long been associated with magic and mystery in many cultures.

The sword Excalibur, which she bestows upon Arthur, symbolises not just kingly power but also the responsibility that comes with it. By accepting the sword from her, Arthur is acknowledging the magical and mysterious forces that underpin his rule.

Superstitions and Beliefs

In Wales, as in many Celtic lands, lakes and other bodies of water have long been associated with magical beings and otherworldly realms. People would leave offerings at lakesides to appease the spirits believed to dwell there. Some of these practises continued well into the Christian era, often blending with newer beliefs.

The Lady of the Lake, as a powerful female figure associated with magic and water, taps into these ancient beliefs. In some parts of Wales, it was believed that fairies or enchantresses could be glimpsed in the mist rising from lakes at dawn or dusk.

There were also superstitions about magical swords hidden in lakes, waiting for the right hero to claim them. These beliefs likely contributed to the enduring popularity of the Excalibur legend.

Connections to Other Myths

The Lady of the Lake shares similarities with water deities and magical women from various mythologies. In Greek myth, the sea nymph Thetis, mother of Achilles, bears some resemblance to her, particularly in her role as a magical mother figure to a great hero.

In Irish mythology, there's a figure known as the Morrígan, a shapeshifting goddess associated with fate, who sometimes appears as a woman washing armour in a river - a harbinger of death in battle. While the Lady of the Lake is generally more benevolent, both figures are powerful feminine presences tied to water and the fates of warriors.

The Welsh figure of Rhiannon, while not specifically associated with water, shares some characteristics with the Lady of the Lake. Both are otherworldly women who play important roles in the stories of great leaders.

The legend of the Lady of the Lake is deeply embedded in the Welsh landscape. Several lakes in Wales claim a connection to her story, each with its own local variations.

Llyn y Fan Fach: Situated in the Brecon Beacons, Llyn y Fan Fach is one such place, renowned for its tale of a magical lake maiden who married a local farmer. According to the legend, she passed on her extensive knowledge of herbal medicine and healing to their sons, who became known as the Physicians of Myddfai.

Llyn Llydaw: Situated in the heart of Snowdonia National Park, Llyn Llydaw lies on the eastern flanks of Snowdon, Wales's highest mountain. This glacial lake, at an elevation of about 440 metres (1,430 feet), is one of the most picturesque in Wales. Its association with the Lady of the Lake likely stems from its dramatic setting and the swirling mists that often shroud the area, creating an atmosphere of mystery and magic. Some local legends suggest that this is where Excalibur was forged and later returned to the lake.

Llyn Ogwen: Also located in Snowdonia, Llyn Ogwen sits in a glacial valley between the Glyderau and Carneddau mountain ranges. This long, narrow lake is surrounded by some of Wales's most imposing peaks, including Tryfan and Pen yr Ole Wen. Local folklore sometimes identifies Llyn Ogwen as the final resting place of King Arthur's sword, Excalibur. The legend states that when Sir Bedivere finally threw the sword into the lake, an arm rose from the waters to catch it – presumably the arm of the Lady of the Lake.

These Welsh lakes, with their dramatic mountainous backdrops and often-misty conditions, provide ideal settings for the mystical elements of Arthurian legend. Their association with the Lady of the Lake speaks to the Welsh tradition of linking landscape features with mythological narratives, a practice that dates back to pre-Christian times.

These stories reflect the profound connection between the Welsh people and their land, particularly its waters. The misty lakes and rain-soaked hills of Wales provide the perfect backdrop for tales of magic and mystery, blending the natural world with the supernatural.

The Lady of the Lake remains one of the most enigmatic and fascinating figures in Arthurian legend. Her story, with its roots in ancient Celtic mythology and its branches spreading through centuries of European literature, continues to captivate audiences worldwide. In Wales, where mist-shrouded lakes still hold an air of mystery, it's easy to imagine a magical lady rising from the waters, bearing gifts of power and prophecy. The enduring appeal of this legend speaks to our fascination with the mysterious, the magical, and the profound connection between the land and its stories.

The Afanc

In the misty lakes of Wales, where the water laps gently against the shore and the mountains cast long shadows, there lurks a creature of legend. The Afanc, a beast as old as the hills themselves, has haunted the imaginations of the Welsh people for centuries. This mythical monster, sometimes described as a crocodile, sometimes as a beaver, and other times as a dwarf-like demon, is said to dwell in the depths of various Welsh lakes, waiting to prey on unsuspecting victims.

The Tale of the Afanc

Long ago, in the heart of Wales, there was a lake known as Llyn Barfog. Its waters were dark and deep, and the locals whispered tales of a terrifying creature that lived beneath its surface. This was the Afanc, a beast so fierce that even the bravest warriors feared to approach the lake's edge.

The Afanc was a curious sight to behold. Some said it had the body of a crocodile, with scales that shimmered like wet stones in the moonlight. Others claimed it looked more like a giant beaver, with powerful teeth that could fell trees and crush bones. And still others insisted it was a demon in the shape of a dwarf, with eyes that glowed like embers in the darkness.

Whatever its true form, the Afanc was a creature of immense strength and cunning. It would lie in wait beneath the water, its eyes just breaking the surface, watching for any unfortunate soul who might come too close to the lake. Then, with a mighty splash and a roar that echoed through the valleys, it would surge forth, dragging its prey down into the murky depths.

The people of the nearby villages lived in constant fear of the Afanc. They warned their children never to go near the lake alone, and even the most seasoned fishermen would not cast their nets in Llyn Barfog. But as the years passed, the Afanc grew bolder. It began to venture out of the lake, causing floods and destruction in the surrounding lands.

The people cried out for help, and their pleas reached the ears of King Arthur himself. The great king, known for his bravery and skill in battle, decided to rid the land of this menace once and for all.

Arthur rode to Llyn Barfog on his mighty steed, determined to face the Afanc. As he approached the lake, the water began to churn and bubble. Suddenly, with a deafening roar, the Afanc burst from the lake, its massive form towering over the king.

But Arthur was not afraid. He had brought with him a long, sturdy chain, forged by the finest smiths in the land. As the Afanc lunged forward, Arthur deftly looped the chain around its neck. Then, urging his horse forward with a shout, he began to drag the beast from its watery home.

The Afanc thrashed and fought, its claws leaving deep gouges in the earth. But Arthur's horse was strong, and inch by inch, the monster was pulled from the lake. As it left the water, the Afanc's strength began to fade. With one final, mighty heave,

Arthur's horse dragged the creature completely onto dry land.

The moment the Afanc was fully out of the water, it let out a terrible shriek. Its body began to shrivel and shrink, until it was no larger than a pebble. Arthur picked up the stone that had once been the fearsome Afanc and cast it far into the mountains, where it could never again threaten the people of Wales.

To this day, near Llyn Barfog, there stands a rock known as Carn March Arthur. It bears a deep groove, said to be the mark left by Arthur's horse as it strained to pull the Afanc from the lake. And though the Afanc is gone, the people of Wales still tell its tale, a reminder of the power of courage in the face of even the most terrifying monsters.

Historical Context and Origins

The legend of the Afanc is deeply rooted in Welsh folklore and mythology. It's a tale that speaks to the ancient relationship between the Welsh people and their landscape, particularly the lakes and waterways that dot the country.

The origins of the Afanc myth likely date back to pre-Christian times, when animistic beliefs were common. These beliefs attributed spirits or souls to natural phenomena, including bodies of water. The Afanc could be seen as a personification of the dangers associated with lakes and rivers – the risk of drowning, flooding, or being swept away by strong currents.

The varied descriptions of the Afanc – from crocodile-like to beaver-like – might reflect the evolution of the myth over time.

The crocodile imagery could be a remnant of stories brought back by travellers who had visited lands where such creatures existed. The beaver-like description is interesting, as beavers were once native to Wales but became extinct there during the 12th century. This could suggest that some versions of the Afanc myth preserve a memory of these long-vanished animals.

The Afanc's habit of causing floods is particularly significant in Welsh history. Many parts of Wales are low-lying and have been prone to flooding throughout history. These floods could be devastating, destroying crops and homes. The Afanc myth provided a supernatural explanation for these natural disasters, giving people a way to understand and talk about these frightening events.

The involvement of figures like King Arthur in some versions of the Afanc legend shows how the myth continued to evolve over time. As Christianity spread through Wales and new stories and heroes became popular, older myths were often adapted and incorporated into these new narratives. This process helped to keep the old stories alive, even as their original meanings might have been lost or changed.

Etymology and Symbolism

The word "Afanc" itself is fascinating from a linguistic perspective. In modern Welsh, "afanc" means "beaver." However, the creature in the myths is clearly something far more fearsome than a simple beaver. This discrepancy might be due to changes in the Welsh language over time, or it might reflect how the nature of the mythical beast changed in people's imaginations.

In some older texts, the creature is referred to as "addanc" rather than "afanc." This variation in spelling and pronunciation is common in oral traditions, where stories are passed down verbally from generation to generation.

Symbolically, the Afanc represents several key themes. As a water-dwelling monster, it embodies the unknown dangers that lurk beneath the surface – not just of lakes and rivers, but of life itself. The Afanc's ability to cause floods symbolises the destructive power of nature, which can upend human lives in an instant.

The various attempts to defeat the Afanc in different versions of the legend often involve trickery or special weapons, suggesting that brute force alone is not enough to overcome life's challenges. This could be seen as a metaphor for the importance of wisdom and cunning in facing difficulties.

Superstitions and Beliefs

The Afanc myth gave rise to various superstitions and beliefs among the Welsh people. Many lakes in Wales were believed to be home to an Afanc, and people would often avoid these bodies of water out of fear.

In some traditions, it was believed that the Afanc would only attack those who entered its lake. This led to the practice of throwing stones into a lake before swimming or fishing, in the hope of driving the Afanc to the furthest shore.

There were also beliefs about how to defeat or control an Afanc. In one tale, a maiden was able to lull the creature to sleep on her lap, allowing others to chain it. This story might have given rise to the belief that Afancs could be pacified by the presence of a pure-hearted woman.

The idea that the Afanc could be made visible using an adder stone (a type of stone with a natural hole through it) reflects the widespread belief in magical objects that could reveal hidden supernatural beings.

Connections to Other Myths

The Afanc shares similarities with other water monsters from mythologies around the world. The Scottish kelpie, a shape-shifting water spirit that often appears as a horse, is another Celtic water monster that lures unsuspecting victims to their doom. The Scandinavian Näcken and the German Nix are other examples of dangerous water spirits from European folklore.

The idea of a flood-causing monster also has parallels in other cultures. In Mesopotamian mythology, for example, the god Enlil sends a flood to destroy humanity, a story that bears similarities to the Biblical flood and Noah's ark.

The tale of King Arthur defeating the Afanc is reminiscent of other hero-versus-monster stories, such as Beowulf's battle with Grendel or Perseus slaying Medusa. These stories often serve as metaphors for humanity's struggle against the forces of chaos and destruction.

The Afanc myth is closely tied to the Welsh landscape. Many lakes in Wales are associated with Afanc legends, including Llyn Barfog, Llyn Llion, and Llyn yr Afanc. These associations have helped to preserve the myth and keep it alive in local folklore.

The story of the Afanc continues to captivate people today. It has been featured in literature, television shows, and even video games, demonstrating its enduring appeal. For the people of Wales, the Afanc remains a powerful symbol of their rich mythological heritage and their deep connection to the land and its waters.

The legend of the Afanc is more than just a scary story about a lake monster. It's a window into the beliefs, fears, and hopes of the Welsh people throughout history. From ancient Celtic beliefs to medieval Arthurian legends, the Afanc has adapted and evolved, much like the culture that created it. Today, it stands as a testament to the enduring power of myth and the profound connection between a people and their land.

Y Ddraig Goch

In the dramatic hills and valleys of Wales, a tale as old as time itself has been passed down through generations. It's a story of two dragons, locked in an epic battle that shook the very foundations of the land. This is the legend of Y Ddraig Goch, the Red Dragon of Wales, a symbol that has come to represent the fierce spirit and proud heritage of the Welsh people.

The Tale of Y Ddraig Goch

Long ago, in a time when magic still danced in the air and mythical creatures roamed the earth, the land that would become Wales was plagued by a terrible problem. Each night, the ground would tremble and shake, causing great distress to the people. King Lludd, the ruler of Britain at the time, was at his wit's end, unable to find the source of this nightly disturbance.

Desperate for a solution, King Lludd sought the counsel of his wise brother, Llefelys. After careful consideration, Llefelys revealed the shocking truth: two dragons, one red and one white, were fighting beneath the earth. Their fierce battle was the cause of the tremors that tormented the land.

Llefelys devised a clever plan to end the dragons' conflict. He instructed King Lludd to dig a deep pit in the very centre of Britain and fill it with mead, the sweet honey wine beloved by gods and mortals alike. Over this pit, a silk cloth was to be spread.

Following his brother's advice, King Lludd set the trap. As night fell, the dragons emerged from their underground lair, drawn by the intoxicating scent of mead. They drank deeply from the pit, their scales glinting in the moonlight as they lapped up the sweet liquid. As the mead worked its magic, the dragons grew drowsy and eventually collapsed onto the silken cloth.

Quick as a flash, King Lludd and his men wrapped the sleeping dragons in the cloth and buried them deep within the earth at Dinas Emrys, a rocky outcrop in Snowdonia. There, they were to remain, locked in their eternal slumber, no longer a threat to the peace of the land.

Years passed, and the dragons faded from memory. But their story was not yet over. Centuries later, King Vortigern attempted to build a castle atop Dinas Emrys. Each night, the walls he built during the day would crumble and fall. Frustrated, Vortigern consulted his advisors, who told him that to break this curse, he must sacrifice a boy with no father at the site.

A young lad named Merlin was brought before the king. But Merlin was no ordinary boy. Gifted with second sight, he revealed the true cause of the falling walls: the two dragons, still sleeping beneath the earth, were stirring.

At Merlin's urging, the ground was excavated, revealing a pool of water. As the pool was drained, two dragons emerged - one red, one white. They immediately resumed their ancient battle, filling the air with roars and the clash of scales.

The white dragon seemed to have the upper hand at first, driving the red dragon to the edge of the pool. But the red dragon fought back with a fierce determination, breathing fire and lashing out with its powerful tail. In a final, climactic struggle, the red dragon overcame its foe, defeating the white dragon once and for all.

Merlin interpreted this battle as a prophecy. The white dragon represented the Saxons, while the red dragon symbolised the native Britons. The red dragon's victory foretold that one day, the Britons would rise up and drive the Saxons from their lands.

From that day forward, the red dragon became a powerful symbol of Welsh identity and resistance. Y Ddraig Goch, the Red Dragon of Wales, took its place on banners and flags, a fierce guardian watching over the Welsh people.

Historical Context and Origins

The legend of Y Ddraig Goch is deeply rooted in Welsh history and folklore. While the tale as we know it today was first recorded in the 9th century in the Historia Brittonum, attributed to the Welsh monk Nennius, its origins likely stretch back much further.

The dragon as a symbol has a long history in Wales and the broader Celtic world. In Celtic mythology, dragons were often associated with sovereignty and kingship. They were seen as guardians of the land and its people, a belief that aligns perfectly with the role of Y Ddraig Goch in Welsh culture.

The story of the battling dragons buried by King Lludd is found in the Mabinogion, a collection of Welsh folktales compiled in the Middle Ages. This version of the tale is believed to be one of the oldest, dating back to ancient Celtic traditions.

The later part of the legend, involving Vortigern and the young Merlin, appears in Geoffrey of Monmouth's Historia Regum Britanniae, written in the 12th century. Geoffrey's work was instrumental in popularising the Arthurian legends and played a significant role in shaping medieval British historiography.

It's worth noting that the historical context of these stories reflects the tumultuous times in which they were set. The conflict between the red and white dragons is often interpreted as an allegory for the struggles between the native Britons and the invading Saxons. This theme of resistance against foreign invaders has been a recurring one in Welsh history and has contributed to the enduring popularity of the Red Dragon as a national symbol.

Etymology and Symbolism

The Welsh name "Y Ddraig Goch" literally translates to "The Red Dragon" in English. The word "draig" in Welsh is related to the Latin "draco" and the Greek "drakon", all meaning "dragon" or "serpent".

The colour red has long been associated with Wales. In Welsh, the colour red is "coch", which is thought to be related to the ancient Celtic word for red, "cocos". Red was a significant colour in Celtic culture, often associated with blood, life force, and vitality.

The dragon itself is a powerful symbol in many cultures around the world. In Western traditions, dragons are often portrayed as fearsome, fire-breathing creatures, while in Eastern cultures, they are typically seen as wise and benevolent. The Welsh dragon seems to embody aspects of both traditions - it is fierce and protective, yet also a symbol of wisdom and sovereignty.

The battle between the red and white dragons is rich in symbolism. Beyond the obvious representation of the conflict between the Britons and the Saxons, it can be seen as a struggle between native and foreign, old and new, or even as an internal conflict within the land itself.

Superstitions and Beliefs

The legend of Y Ddraig Goch has given rise to various superstitions and beliefs over the centuries. Some of these include:

- The belief that the red dragon would protect Wales from invasion
- The idea that sighting a red dragon was a sign of good fortune
- The superstition that wearing or displaying the image of the red dragon would bring strength and courage

In some parts of Wales, it was once believed that dragons lived in caves and mountain lairs. People would leave offerings at these sites to appease the dragons and ensure good fortune.

The association of dragons with wisdom and prophecy, as seen in the character of Merlin in the legend, also led to the belief that dragons possessed magical knowledge. This idea persisted in Welsh folklore long after the Christianisation of the region.

Connections to Other Myths

The Welsh dragon myth shares similarities with dragon legends from other cultures:

- In English folklore, Saint George slays a dragon, symbolising the triumph of Christianity over paganism
- Norse mythology features the dragon Nidhogg, who gnaws at the roots of the world tree Yggdrasil
- Chinese mythology reveres dragons as symbols of imperial power and good fortune

The theme of buried or sleeping dragons is also found in other cultures. In English legend, the dragons of Unsworth are said to sleep beneath the earth, much like the dragons at Dinas Emrys.

The prophecy element of the Welsh dragon tale also has parallels in other mythologies. In Greek myth, the Oracle of Delphi made prophecies that often influenced the course of history, much like Merlin's interpretation of the dragon battle.

Y Ddraig Goch in Welsh Culture

The red dragon has become an integral part of Welsh national identity. It appears on the national flag of Wales, adopted officially in 1959, although its use as a Welsh symbol dates back much further.

The dragon features prominently in Welsh heraldry and has been used by Welsh rulers for centuries. Owen Glyndŵr, the last native Welshman to hold the title Prince of Wales, used the dragon on his banner during his revolt against English rule in the early 15th century.

Today, the red dragon can be seen throughout Wales - on government buildings, sports jerseys, and countless souvenirs. It's a proud symbol of Welsh heritage and identity, a constant reminder of the country's rich history and enduring spirit.

The legend of Y Ddraig Goch is more than just a myth - it's a powerful symbol of Welsh identity and resilience. From its ancient origins to its place on the modern Welsh flag, the red dragon continues to inspire and unite the people of Wales. It serves as a link to the past, a guardian of the present, and a beacon of hope for the future. In the rolling hills and misty valleys of Wales, the spirit of Y Ddraig Goch lives on, as fierce and proud as ever.

The Tylwyth Teg

Whispers of magical beings have echoed for centuries throughout Wales. These enchanting creatures, known as the Tylwyth Teg, have captivated the imaginations of the Welsh people, weaving their way into the fabric of folklore and tradition. Let's journey into the realm of these fascinating fairy folk and uncover the secrets they hold.

The Tale of the Tylwyth Teg

In a small village nestled in the heart of Wales, young Elin lived with her parents in a cosy cottage near the edge of an ancient forest. Elin was known for her golden hair that shimmered like sunbeams, a feature that caught the eye of more than just the villagers.

One misty evening, as Elin's mother tucked her into bed, she warned, "Remember, love, never wander into the forest at night. The Tylwyth Teg roam there, and they have a fondness for pretty children with hair like yours."

Elin nodded, but curiosity burned in her young heart. As the moon rose high in the sky, she heard the faint sound of laughter and music drifting from the woods. Unable to resist, she slipped out of bed and tiptoed towards the forest.

At the edge of the trees, Elin gasped in wonder. A group of beautiful, fair-haired beings danced in a perfect circle, their feet barely touching the grass. Their clothes sparkled like dewdrops in the moonlight, and their voices were as sweet as birdsong.

One of the Tylwyth Teg, a woman with hair as golden as Elin's, spotted the child and beckoned her with a smile. "Come, little one," she said, her voice like honey. "Dance with us."

Elin took a step forward, enchanted. But just as she was about to enter the fairy ring, she remembered her mother's warning. With great effort, she turned and ran back to her cottage, her heart pounding.

The next morning, Elin's mother found a gift on their doorstep - a wreath of flowers that never wilted. It was a blessing from the Tylwyth Teg, a thank you for the respect Elin had shown by resisting their call.

From that day on, Elin's family always left a bowl of milk outside their door at night, a gesture of goodwill towards their magical neighbours. In return, their cottage was blessed with good fortune, their crops thrived, and their livestock remained healthy.

As Elin grew older, she shared this tale with her own children, ensuring that the legend of the Tylwyth Teg lived on, a cherished part of their Welsh heritage.

Historical Context and Origins

The Tylwyth Teg have been a part of Welsh folklore for centuries, their stories passed down through generations. The term "tylwyth teg" first appeared in writing in the 14th century, in a poem by the renowned Welsh bard Dafydd ap Gwilym. In this poem, a character loses his way while trying to visit his girlfriend, suggesting that even then, the Tylwyth Teg were associated with leading travellers astray.

These fairy folk are deeply rooted in the Celtic traditions of Wales. They share similarities with the Aos Sí of Irish folklore, reflecting the shared cultural heritage of these Celtic nations. The belief in these magical beings was once widespread throughout Wales, particularly in rural areas where the natural landscape - with its mysterious forests, misty mountains, and hidden valleys - provided the perfect setting for tales of the supernatural.

In Welsh society, the Tylwyth Teg served multiple purposes. They were used to explain natural phenomena, to teach moral lessons, and to provide a sense of wonder and magic in everyday life. Parents might use stories of the Tylwyth Teg to keep children from wandering too far from home, while farmers might attribute a good harvest to the blessings of these fairy folk.

The Tylwyth Teg were not always seen as benevolent beings. Like many fairy creatures in folklore around the world, they could be capricious and even dangerous. This dual nature reflected the Welsh people's complex relationship with the natural world - both reliant on its bounty and wary of its dangers.

The name "Tylwyth Teg" itself is rich with meaning. In Middle Welsh, it translates to "Fair Family," reflecting the belief that these beings were not only beautiful but also part of a complex social structure, much like human families.

Other names for these fairy folk include "Bendith y Mamau," meaning "Blessing of the Mothers." This name hints at a connection to fertility and motherhood, suggesting that the Tylwyth Teg might have once been associated with nature goddesses or mother figures in pre-Christian Welsh beliefs.

The Tylwyth Teg's association with gold - both in their own appearance and their desire for golden-haired children - is symbolically significant. Gold has long been associated with the sun, divinity, and immortality in many cultures. The Tylwyth Teg's golden hair might represent their otherworldly, immortal nature.

The fairy rings in which the Tylwyth Teg dance are also deeply symbolic. Circles have long been associated with eternity and magic in many cultures. In Welsh folklore, these rings were seen as gateways between our world and the realm of the fairies.

Superstitions and Beliefs

Many superstitions and beliefs surrounded the Tylwyth Teg in traditional Welsh culture:

- **Leaving out milk**: It was common practice to leave a bowl of milk out for the Tylwyth Teg at night. This was seen as a way to gain their favour and avoid their mischief.

- **Fairy rings**: Circular patterns in grass or mushrooms were believed to be caused by fairy dances. It was considered dangerous to step inside these rings, as one might be trapped in the fairy realm.

- **Changeling children**: The Tylwyth Teg were believed to sometimes steal human babies, leaving changelings in their place. Parents would look out for signs that their child had been swapped, such as unusual behaviour or physical changes.

- **Iron**: Like many fairy creatures in European folklore, the Tylwyth Teg were believed to be vulnerable to iron. Keeping iron items around the house or on one's person was thought to ward off fairy mischief.

- **Fairy gold**: The Tylwyth Teg were sometimes said to bestow riches on humans, but this fairy gold would turn to leaves or dirt if spoken about.

- **Fairy wives**: Stories told of Tylwyth Teg women marrying human men, but these marriages were always fragile, often ending when the fairy wife came into contact with iron.

Connections to Other Myths

The Tylwyth Teg share many characteristics with fairy folk from other cultures. Their love of dancing and music is reminiscent of the Irish sidhe, while their habit of leading travellers astray is similar to the will-o'-the-wisp found in

British folklore.

The concept of changelings is found in many European folklores, from Ireland to Scandinavia. Similarly, the idea of fairy rings is widespread, appearing in British, Irish, German, and Scandinavian myths among others.

The Tylwyth Teg's vulnerability to iron is a trait shared by many supernatural creatures in European folklore, possibly reflecting the cultural shift that occurred with the Iron Age.

The various types of Tylwyth Teg described by folklorist Wirt Sikes - such as the mine-dwelling Coblynau and the household Bwbachod - have counterparts in other cultures. The Coblynau, for instance, are similar to the Cornish knockers or the German kobolds, while the Bwbachod share characteristics with the Scottish brownie.

The Tylwyth Teg in the Welsh Landscape

The stories of the Tylwyth Teg are intimately tied to the Welsh landscape. These fairy folk were said to inhabit the wild and untamed parts of Wales - the deep forests, misty mountains, and hidden lakes that have long captured the Welsh imagination.

Certain locations in Wales are particularly associated with the Tylwyth Teg. The lakes of Snowdonia, for instance, are said to be home to the Gwragedd Annwn, the female water fairies. The old copper and gold mines of Wales were believed to be the domain of the Coblynau.

Even today, visitors to Wales might hear stories of fairy sightings or unexplained phenomena attributed to the Tylwyth Teg. While belief in these beings may have waned, their presence in Welsh culture remains strong, a testament to the enduring power of folklore and the deep connection between the Welsh people and their magical landscape.

The Tylwyth Teg, with their golden hair and ethereal beauty, continue to enchant us today. These fairy folk represent more than just magical beings - they embody the rich cultural heritage of Wales, the deep connection between the Welsh people and their land, and the enduring power of storytelling.

The presence of the Tylwyth Teg can still be felt in Wales. Their stories remind us of a time when the line between the magical and the mundane was less clearly drawn, when every hill and stream might hide a wonder.

The Tylwyth Teg may be creatures of myth, but the truths they represent - the importance of respect for nature, the power of kindness, the wonder of the unknown - are very real indeed.

So the next time you find yourself in a quiet Welsh forest or by a still mountain lake, take a moment to listen. You might just hear the faint laughter of the Tylwyth Teg, dancing their eternal dance just beyond our sight.

Cantre'r Gwaelod

Along the western coast of Wales, where the lapping waves of Cardigan Bay meet the shore, lies a tale as old as the hills themselves. It's a story of a land lost to the sea, a kingdom submerged beneath the waters, known as Cantre'r Gwaelod. This legend, often called the "Welsh Atlantis," has captivated the hearts and minds of the Welsh people for centuries, weaving its way into their folklore, literature, and songs.

The Tale of Cantre'r Gwaelod

Long ago, in a time when the world was young and magic still danced in the air, there existed a beautiful and bountiful land called Cantre'r Gwaelod. This kingdom stretched far out into what is now Cardigan Bay, its fertile fields and lush forests reaching from Ramsey Island in the south to Bardsey Island in the north.

The people of Cantre'r Gwaelod lived happy and prosperous lives, protected from the hungry sea by a great dyke known as Sarn Badrig. This mighty wall stood tall and strong, guarding the low-lying lands from the relentless waves. At its heart stood sixteen sturdy gates, which were opened at low tide to drain the land and closed at high tide to keep the waters at bay.

The capital of this wondrous realm was Caer Wyddno, a grand city ruled by the wise King Gwyddno Garanhir. The king had entrusted the care of the dyke to Prince Seithenyn, known for his love of merrymaking and drink.

One fateful night, as a great storm brewed over the Irish Sea, the kingdom held a grand feast. The wind howled and the waves crashed against Sarn Badrig, but the people of Cantre'r Gwaelod paid no heed, for they trusted in the strength of their dyke and the vigilance of Prince Seithenyn.

But alas, the prince had indulged too deeply in the pleasures of the feast. His head clouded by wine and song, he neglected his duty to check the gates. As the storm raged on, the sea rose higher and higher, until at last it breached the unmanned defences.

In the dark of night, a watchman named Teithi Hen noticed the rising waters and ran to sound the alarm. He raced through the streets of Caer Wyddno, crying out for all to flee to higher ground. Many heeded his warning and scrambled to safety, but many more were lost to the hungry sea.

As dawn broke, where once stood the fair kingdom of Cantre'r Gwaelod, there was nothing but the rolling waves of Cardigan Bay. The land had vanished beneath the waters, swallowed by the sea due to one man's carelessness.

It's said that on quiet nights, when the moon is full and the tide is low, one can still hear the mournful tolling of the bells of Cantre'r Gwaelod, ringing out from beneath the waves to warn of approaching danger.

The legend of Cantre'r Gwaelod has deep roots in Welsh folklore, with its earliest known written reference appearing in the Black Book of Carmarthen, a manuscript dating back to the 13th century. In this early version, the land is referred to as Maes Gwyddno (Gwyddno's Field) and its loss is attributed to the negligence of a well-maiden named Mererid.

Over time, the story evolved and grew more complex. By the 17th century, it had taken on many of the elements we recognize today, including the dyke of Sarn Badrig and the character of Prince Seithenyn.

The tale of Cantre'r Gwaelod isn't just a flight of fancy, though. It likely has its roots in real geological events. Following the last ice age, sea levels rose dramatically, flooding low-lying coastal areas. This gradual inundation would have been observed and remembered by the people living in these regions, passing from generation to generation as stories of lost lands.

Evidence of this ancient landscape can still be seen today. At Ynyslas, near Borth, the remains of a submerged forest are visible at low tide, its ancient tree stumps a stark reminder of a time when the sea lay much further out. Archaeologists have also discovered human artefacts in places like Sarn Gynfelyn, suggesting that people once lived and worked in areas now claimed by the sea.

Recent research using medieval maps has even hinted at possible remnants of this lost land still existing beneath the waves of Cardigan Bay. While these findings don't prove the existence of Cantre'r Gwaelod as described in legend, they do show that the story may have more basis in fact than previously thought.

Etymology and Symbolism

The name Cantre'r Gwaelod itself is rich with meaning. In Welsh, "Cantref" (or Cantre) refers to an administrative division of land, while "Gwaelod" means "bottom" or "low-lying." So, Cantre'r Gwaelod can be translated as "The Lowland Hundred," aptly describing its geographical nature.

The characters in the tale also carry symbolic weight. King Gwyddno Garanhir's name translates to "Gwyddno Long-Shanks," perhaps suggesting his ability to wade through the flooded lands. Prince Seithenyn, whose negligence leads to the kingdom's downfall, represents the dangers of excess and the importance of responsibility.

The dyke, Sarn Badrig (Saint Patrick's Causeway), symbolises the thin line between safety and disaster, while its sixteen gates represent human control over nature - a control that proves fragile in the face of natural forces.

Superstitions and Beliefs

The legend of Cantre'r Gwaelod has given rise to various superstitions and beliefs along the Welsh coast. Many locals believe that on calm nights, the bells of the submerged churches can be heard ringing beneath the waves, warning of impending storms or danger.

This belief is so strong that it inspired the Welsh folk song "Clychau Aberdyfi" (The Bells of Aberdovey), which tells of the sunken bells and their eerie music. The legend has become such a part of local identity that the village of Aberdyfi has incorporated it into their school emblem.

Some fishermen in Cardigan Bay still claim to see glimpses of ancient buildings or roads beneath the water on particularly clear days. While these sightings are likely natural formations, they speak to the enduring power of the Cantre'r Gwaelod myth in the local imagination.

Connections to Other Myths

The story of Cantre'r Gwaelod is not unique to Wales. Similar tales of sunken lands can be found across Celtic mythology and beyond. In Brittany, there's the legend of the city of Ker-Ys, also swallowed by the sea due to human failings. In Cornwall, the mythical land of Lyonesse is said to lie beneath the waves between Land's End and the Isles of Scilly.

These stories share common themes: a prosperous land, human negligence or sin, and ultimate destruction by the sea. They often serve as cautionary tales about the dangers of hubris and the importance of respecting nature's power.

The flooding motif isn't limited to Celtic mythology either. From the Biblical story of Noah's Ark to the ancient Mesopotamian Epic of Gilgamesh, tales of great floods destroying civilizations appear in cultures worldwide. This universality suggests that such stories may have origins in actual events, perhaps memories of post-ice age sea level rises or catastrophic local floods.

Geological Evidence and Modern Interpretations

While the legend of Cantre'r Gwaelod is clearly mythical in many aspects, it may contain kernels of truth. Geologists have found evidence of significant changes in the coastline of Cardigan Bay over thousands of years.

The sarnau, or causeways, that stretch out into Cardigan Bay (including Sarn Badrig) are now known to be natural formations - glacial moraines left behind by retreating ice sheets. However, their existence likely contributed to the development of the Cantre'r Gwaelod myth, as they appear to be man-made structures stretching out towards the supposed location of the sunken kingdom.

Modern archaeology and geology have revealed that the area now covered by Cardigan Bay was indeed dry land after the last ice age, gradually flooding as sea levels rose. This slow inundation would have been observed by the inhabitants of the time, potentially giving rise to stories of lost lands that were passed down through generations.

The legend of Cantre'r Gwaelod continues to captivate imaginations and inspire creativity. It has featured in literature, from medieval Welsh poetry to modern children's books. Artists have painted its imagined landscapes, and musicians have sung of its sunken bells.

More than just a story, Cantre'r Gwaelod represents the deep connection between the Welsh people and their land. It speaks to the respect and fear they hold for the sea that shapes their shores, and serves as a reminder of the impermanence of human works in the face of nature's power.

As we look out over the waters of Cardigan Bay today, we're reminded that beneath those waves lies not just sand and stone, but layer upon layer of history and myth. The story of Cantre'r Gwaelod invites us to imagine what once was, and what might have been, in this ancient land of Wales.

Lleu Llaw Gyffes

In the hills and valleys of Wales, where ancient stories whisper on the wind, there's a tale of a hero unlike any other. This is the story of Lleu Llaw Gyffes, a figure of Welsh mythology whose life was filled with magic, betrayal, and triumph. His tale is woven into the fabric of Welsh culture, a reminder of the rich history and folklore that shapes the land to this day.

The Tale of Lleu Llaw Gyffes

Long ago, in the kingdom of Gwynedd, there lived a powerful magician named Math fab Mathonwy. Math could only live if his feet rested in the lap of a maiden, except when he was at war. His foot-holder was a beautiful young woman named Goewin.

Math had a nephew named Gwydion, who was also skilled in magic. Gwydion's brother, Gilfaethwy, fell in love with Goewin and became consumed with desire for her. To help his brother, Gwydion hatched a plan to distract Math with a war, allowing Gilfaethwy to be alone with Goewin.

Their scheme worked, but at a terrible cost. Gilfaethwy raped Goewin, and when Math discovered this, he was furious. As punishment, he used his magic to transform Gwydion and Gilfaethwy into animals. For three years, they lived as different mated pairs - deer, pigs, and wolves - giving birth to offspring each year.

After their punishment ended, Gwydion and Gilfaethwy returned to their human forms. Math, needing a new foot-holder, asked his sister Arianrhod to take on the role. But first, he tested her virtue by making her step over his magic wand. As she did so, she suddenly gave birth to two children - a boy named Dylan, who immediately ran off to the sea, and a small something that Gwydion quickly scooped up and hid in a chest.

Arianrhod, shamed by this revelation, fled from Math's court. Gwydion took care of the small being he had hidden, and it grew quickly into a handsome boy. When Gwydion presented the child to Arianrhod, she was angry and placed three curses, or tynghedau, on the boy:

1. That only she could give him a name.
2. That only she could give him arms.
3. That he would never have a human wife.

Gwydion, determined to help the boy, used his cunning to trick Arianrhod into naming the child Lleu Llaw Gyffes, meaning "The Fair-Haired One with the Skillful Hand." Later, he disguised himself and Lleu as shoemakers and tricked Arianrhod into arming Lleu when their camp was threatened by a magical army Gwydion had conjured.

To overcome the third curse, Gwydion and Math used their magic to create a wife for Lleu from the flowers of oak, broom, and meadowsweet. They named her Blodeuwedd, which means "Flower-Face."

Lleu and Blodeuwedd lived happily for a time, but tragedy was brewing. While Lleu was away, Blodeuwedd fell in love with a hunter named Gronw Pebr. The two plotted to kill Lleu, but because of his magical nature, he could only be killed in very specific circumstances - while he was neither inside nor outside, neither on horseback nor on foot, and with a spear that had been crafted over the course of a year, but only when people were attending Mass on Sundays.

Blodeuwedd tricked Lleu into revealing how he could be killed, and then created those exact circumstances. Gronw threw the spear at Lleu, but instead of dying, Lleu transformed into an eagle and flew away.

Gwydion searched far and wide for Lleu, finally finding him perched in a tree, his flesh rotting and falling to the ground. With a magical song, Gwydion lured Lleu down and restored him to his human form.

In revenge, Lleu killed Gronw with the same spear that had wounded him. As for Blodeuwedd, Gwydion transformed her into an owl, doomed to be hated by all other birds.

With his trials behind him, Lleu took his rightful place as the ruler of Gwynedd, bringing peace and prosperity to the land.

Historical Context and Origins

The tale of Lleu Llaw Gyffes is part of the Fourth Branch of the Mabinogi, a collection of Welsh myths and legends that were written down in the Middle Ages but likely existed in oral tradition for centuries before. These stories give us a glimpse into the beliefs, values, and social structures of medieval Wales.

The Mabinogi was first written down in Welsh sometime between 1050 and 1225. The stories blend elements of Celtic mythology with influences from the medieval court culture of Wales. They reflect a society in transition, caught between ancient pagan traditions and the growing influence of Christianity.

Lleu's story, in particular, showcases the importance of magic and shapeshifting in Welsh mythology. The ability to change form - whether it's Gwydion and Gilfaethwy becoming animals, Lleu turning into an eagle, or Blodeuwedd being transformed from flowers to a woman to an owl - is a common theme in Celtic myths.

The tale also reflects the complex family dynamics and power struggles of medieval Welsh society. The importance of lineage and inheritance is clear in Lleu's eventual rise to power, while the betrayal by Blodeuwedd might reflect anxieties about marriage alliances and loyalty in a society where political power often depended on such relationships.

Etymology and Symbolism

The name Lleu is thought to come from the Proto-Celtic Lugus, a widely worshipped god in the ancient Celtic world. Scholars have debated the exact meaning of the name, with suggestions ranging from "light" to "oath" or even "raven."

Lleu's epithet, Llaw Gyffes, means "Skillful Hand" in Welsh, possibly referring to his prowess as a warrior or craftsman.

This ties into the wider Indo-European tradition of sky gods associated with oaths, craftsmanship, and kingship.

The symbolism in Lleu's story is rich and multi-layered. His transformation into an eagle might symbolise his divine nature or his role as a sky god. The specific circumstances of his near-death - being neither inside nor outside, neither mounted nor on foot - reflect the liminal nature of divine figures who exist between worlds.

Blodeuwedd, created from flowers, represents the connection between nature and humanity in Welsh mythology. Her transformation into an owl symbolises betrayal and the consequences of going against one's nature.

Superstitions and Beliefs

The story of Lleu Llaw Gyffes is tied to several superstitions and beliefs that were common in medieval Wales:

- The power of curses or tynghedau: The belief that words, especially those spoken by someone with power or authority, could shape a person's destiny.

- The magical properties of plants: The creation of Blodeuwedd from flowers reflects the belief in the magical properties of nature.

- Shapeshifting: The ability to change form was often associated with magical or divine beings in Welsh folklore.

- The sacredness of oaths: The specific conditions for Lleu's death highlight the importance of oaths and the consequences of breaking them.

- The owl as a symbol of betrayal: After her transformation, Blodeuwedd as an owl was said to be hated by all other birds, reflecting the belief that owls were associated with betrayal and ill omens.

Connections to Other Myths

Lleu Llaw Gyffes shares many similarities with other figures in Celtic mythology:

- He is often compared to the Irish god Lugh and the Gaulish Lugus, both of whom were associated with light, skill, and kingship.

- His magical birth and rapid growth are similar to other "wonder child" figures in Celtic myths, such as Cú Chulainn in Irish legend.

- The creation of Blodeuwedd from flowers is reminiscent of the Greek myth of Pygmalion, where a statue comes to life.

- Lleu's specific vulnerabilities recall other mythological figures who could only be killed under certain circumstances, such as Achilles in Greek mythology or Baldr in Norse myths.

The Landscape of Lleu's Tale

The story of Lleu is deeply rooted in the Welsh landscape. The kingdom of Gwynedd, where much of the action takes place, is in north-west Wales, a region of rugged mountains, deep valleys, and misty forests. This dramatic scenery forms the backdrop to Lleu's magical adventures.

Specific locations mentioned in the tale include:

- Dinas Dinlleu, a hill fort near Caernarfon, which is said to have been Lleu's court.
- Nantlleu, a valley in Gwynedd, whose name means "Lleu's Stream."
- Bryn Cyfergyr, where Lleu was struck by Gronw's spear.

These places still exist today, tying the ancient myth to the modern Welsh landscape and keeping the legend of Lleu alive in the cultural memory of Wales.

The tale of Lleu Llaw Gyffes is more than just a story - it's a window into the rich cultural heritage of Wales. From the misty hills of Gwynedd to the magical transformations and betrayals, Lleu's story captures the essence of Welsh mythology. It reminds us of the power of storytelling to connect us with our past, our land, and our shared human experiences. As long as these tales are told, the magic of ancient Wales will continue to inspire and enchant new generations.

Blodeuwedd

In the mystical past of Wales, where magic and nature intertwine, there's a story that's been whispered for generations. It's a tale of love, betrayal, and transformation that speaks to the very heart of Welsh mythology. This is the story of Blodeuwedd, the woman made of flowers, whose fate became as changeable as the seasons themselves.

The Tale of Blodeuwedd

Long ago, in the green valleys of Wales, there lived a powerful magician named Math and his clever nephew, Gwydion. They were known far and wide for their magical abilities, but even they were put to the test when faced with a peculiar problem.

Lleu Llaw Gyffes, a young man of great potential, had been cursed never to have a human wife. This curse weighed heavily on Lleu, for he longed for companionship and love. Math and Gwydion, determined to help, put their heads together and came up with a plan as wild as the Welsh countryside itself.

On a warm spring day, when the flowers were in full bloom, Math and Gwydion ventured into the lush meadows. With a wave of their wands and a few magic words, they began to gather the most beautiful blooms - the sturdy oak, the vibrant broom, and the sweet-smelling meadowsweet. As they wove their spell, the flowers began to twist and turn, taking on a new shape.

Before their very eyes, a woman of extraordinary beauty emerged from the blossoms. Her hair was as golden as the broom, her skin as soft as oak leaves, and her scent as sweet as meadowsweet. They named her Blodeuwedd, which means "Flower-Face" in Welsh.

Lleu was overjoyed when he met Blodeuwedd. Her beauty and grace captivated him, and soon they were married. For a time, they lived happily in their home in the Welsh mountains, and it seemed that Lleu's curse had truly been broken.

But Blodeuwedd, born of flowers, was as changeable as the seasons. While Lleu was away, she met a handsome hunter named Gronw Pebr. The two fell deeply in love, and Blodeuwedd's heart turned away from Lleu.

Knowing that Lleu was protected by powerful magic, Blodeuwedd and Gronw hatched a plan. She coaxed the secret of Lleu's vulnerability from him, learning that he could only be killed in a very specific way - while standing with one foot on a bath and one on a goat, struck by a spear that had been crafted over the course of a year, and only on Sundays.

With this knowledge, Blodeuwedd and Gronw set their plan in motion. They created the exact conditions Lleu had described, and Gronw threw the spear. But as it struck Lleu, something extraordinary happened. Instead of falling dead, Lleu transformed into an eagle and flew away, grievously wounded.

Gwydion, hearing of this betrayal, set out to find Lleu. After a long search, he discovered the injured eagle and used his magic to restore Lleu to his human form. Filled with anger and hurt, Lleu sought revenge.

Blodeuwedd, hearing of Lleu's return, fled into the forest. Gwydion pursued her, and when he caught up, he used his magic once more. This time, he transformed Blodeuwedd into an owl, condemning her to live alone and be shunned by other birds.

Gronw, for his part, offered to make amends by allowing Lleu to throw a spear at him. He asked only to place a large stone between them. Lleu agreed, but his throw was so powerful that it pierced the stone and killed Gronw.

And so, the tale of Blodeuwedd came to an end. The woman made of flowers became a creature of the night, forever changed by love, betrayal, and magic. To this day, in the quiet Welsh nights, you might hear the hoot of an owl and wonder if it's Blodeuwedd, still wandering the forests of her homeland.

Historical Context and Origins

The story of Blodeuwedd is part of the Fourth Branch of the Mabinogi, a collection of Welsh myths and legends that form the cornerstone of Welsh mythology. These tales, passed down through oral tradition for centuries, were finally written down in the Middle Ages, preserving them for future generations.

The Mabinogi provides a window into the beliefs, values, and social structures of medieval Wales. The tale of Blodeuwedd, in particular, reflects the complex relationships between men and women, the power of magic, and the consequences of betrayal in Welsh society.

The creation of Blodeuwedd by Math and Gwydion showcases the belief in powerful magic and the ability to create life from natural elements. This reflects the deep connection between Welsh people and their natural surroundings, a relationship that has been central to Welsh culture for millennia.

The setting of the story in the mountains of Wales is significant. The Welsh landscape, with its rugged mountains, deep valleys, and dense forests, has always played a crucial role in shaping Welsh mythology. These natural features were often seen as the dwelling places of magical beings and the backdrop for supernatural events.

The transformation of Blodeuwedd into an owl is particularly interesting from a historical perspective. Owls have long held a special place in Welsh folklore, often associated with wisdom but also with death and the otherworld. By turning Blodeuwedd into an owl, the story ties into existing beliefs about these nocturnal birds.

Etymology and Symbolism

The name Blodeuwedd itself is rich with meaning. In Welsh, "blodeu" means flowers, and "gwedd" can be translated as face or aspect. So, Blodeuwedd literally means "flower face" or "flower aspect," reflecting her origins as a woman created from flowers.

The choice of flowers used to create Blodeuwedd is also

symbolic:

- **Oak**: Represents strength and endurance. In many cultures, including Welsh, the oak is seen as a sacred tree.
- **Broom**: Known for its bright yellow flowers, broom symbolises humility and purity.
- **Meadowsweet**: This sweet-smelling flower is associated with love and grace.

These flowers combined suggest a being of strength, beauty, and love - all qualities that Blodeuwedd embodies in her human form.

The transformation of Blodeuwedd into an owl carries its own symbolism. In Welsh tradition, the owl is often associated with wisdom, but also with deception and death. This transformation can be seen as a punishment that fits Blodeuwedd's crime - her deception leads to her becoming a creature associated with deception.

Superstitions and Beliefs

The tale of Blodeuwedd has given rise to several superstitions and beliefs in Welsh culture:

- It's considered bad luck to harm or kill an owl, as it might be Blodeuwedd or one of her descendants.
- The call of an owl at night is sometimes seen as a warning of impending betrayal or deceit.
- In some parts of Wales, meadowsweet is still known as "Blodeuwedd's flower" and is believed to have magical properties.

The story also reinforces the Welsh belief in the power of magic and the idea that the natural world is filled with hidden wonders and dangers.

Connections to Other Myths

The story of Blodeuwedd shares themes with myths from other cultures:

- The creation of a woman from flowers is reminiscent of the Greek myth of Pygmalion, where a sculptor creates a woman from ivory.
- The theme of a magical wife betraying her husband appears in the Irish legend of Étaín, who, like Blodeuwedd, is associated with butterflies and transformation.
- The transformation of humans into animals as punishment is a common theme in Greek mythology, such as the story of Arachne being turned into a spider.

Blodeuwedd in the Welsh Landscape

The tale of Blodeuwedd is deeply rooted in the Welsh landscape. The mountains where Lleu and Blodeuwedd lived are often identified as Moel Hebog in Gwynedd, North Wales. This connection to real places helps to anchor the myth in the physical world, making it feel more immediate and real to the people of Wales.

The flowers used to create Blodeuwedd - oak, broom, and meadowsweet - are all native to Wales and can still be found growing wild in the Welsh countryside. This further reinforces the story's connection to the land and its natural beauty.

The transformation of Blodeuwedd into an owl ties the story to the nocturnal soundscape of Wales. The hooting of owls in the Welsh forests at night serves as a constant reminder of this ancient tale.

The story of Blodeuwedd continues to captivate people today, centuries after it was first told. It speaks to timeless themes of love, betrayal, and the consequences of our actions. More than that, it serves as a link to the rich mythology of Wales, a reminder of the magic that our ancestors saw in the world around them.

In the misty valleys and atop the rugged mountains of Wales, one can still feel the echoes of this ancient tale. The flowers still bloom, the owls still hoot, and somewhere, perhaps, the spirit of Blodeuwedd still roams, a testament to the enduring power of Welsh mythology.

Merlin

In ancient Wales, where magic whispers through the air and legends are born from the very earth, there lived a man whose name would echo through the ages. This is the story of Merlin, the most famous wizard in world folklore, whose wisdom and powers shaped the destiny of kings and kingdoms.

The Tale of Merlin

Long ago, in a small village nestled among the lush green valleys of Wales, a child was born unlike any other. His mother was a mortal woman, but his father, it was said, was an incubus - a spirit of the air. This unusual parentage gifted the boy with extraordinary abilities that would one day change the course of history.

As a lad, Merlin showed signs of his magical nature. He could see things others couldn't, speak with animals, and even predict the future. The villagers whispered about him, some in awe, others in fear. But Merlin paid them no mind, for he knew his destiny lay beyond the boundaries of his humble beginnings.

As he grew older, Merlin's fame spread throughout the land. Kings and warriors sought his counsel, for his wisdom was as deep as the roots of the ancient oaks. It was during this time that he met the young Arthur, a boy destined to become the greatest king Britain had ever known.

Merlin took Arthur under his wing, teaching him the ways of leadership and the importance of justice. Using his magic, Merlin arranged for Arthur to pull the legendary sword Excalibur from the stone, proving his right to rule.

For many years, Merlin stood by Arthur's side, guiding him through battles and political strife. He helped establish the Round Table, where knights of valour gathered to serve the king and protect the realm.

But even the greatest of wizards can't escape the pitfalls of the heart. Merlin fell in love with a beautiful and clever woman named Nimue, also known as the Lady of the Lake. He taught her his magical secrets, not realising that she would use this knowledge against him.

In a twist of fate, Nimue used Merlin's own magic to trap him. Some say she imprisoned him in a crystal cave, others in an oak tree. Whatever the case, Merlin vanished from the world of men, leaving behind a legacy that would inspire stories for centuries to come.

Historical Context and Origins

The tale of Merlin is deeply rooted in Welsh folklore, but its popularity spread far beyond the borders of Wales. The character we know today is a blend of several legendary figures, including the Welsh prophet Myrddin Wyllt and the Roman-British war leader Ambrosius Aurelianus.

The earliest written accounts of Merlin come from the 12th century, penned by the Welsh writer Geoffrey of Monmouth. In his work "Historia Regum Britanniae" (History of the Kings of Britain), Geoffrey combined these earlier legends to create Merlinus Ambrosius, the character who would become the foundation for all future versions of Merlin.

Geoffrey's Merlin was a powerful prophet and magician who played a crucial role in the story of King Arthur. This version of the tale quickly gained popularity, especially in Wales, where it resonated with local traditions and beliefs.

In the 13th century, French writers like Robert de Boron further developed Merlin's character. They added new elements to his story, such as his demonic parentage and his role in Arthur's conception. These additions gave Merlin a more complex backstory and tied him even more closely to the Arthurian legend.

Etymology and Symbolism

The name "Merlin" itself has an interesting history. It comes from the Welsh "Myrddin," which Geoffrey of Monmouth Latinized to "Merlinus." This change was likely made to avoid any unfortunate associations with the Anglo-Norman French word "merde" (meaning dung).

The name has been interpreted in various ways. Some link it to the Welsh word for sea fortress, while others connect it to the word for madman. These different interpretations reflect the multifaceted nature of Merlin's character - a wise advisor, a powerful magician, and sometimes a wild prophet.

Merlin's character is rich in symbolism. As a cambion

(half-human, half-demon), he represents the blending of the mortal and supernatural worlds. His ability to shapeshift symbolises the fluid nature of reality and the power of transformation.

His role as Arthur's advisor symbolises the importance of wisdom and foresight in leadership. Merlin's magic often serves as a metaphor for the power of knowledge and the ability to see beyond the obvious.

Superstitions and Beliefs

Many superstitions and beliefs grew up around the figure of Merlin. In some parts of Wales, it was believed that Merlin's spirit still roamed the forests, ready to offer guidance to those pure of heart.

Some believed that Merlin had the power to control the weather, and sailors would invoke his name for safe passage. Others thought that carrying a sprig of oak (associated with Merlin due to his imprisonment in an oak tree) would bring wisdom and protection.

There were also those who believed that Merlin's prophecies were still coming true, and they scrutinised current events for signs of his predictions. This belief persisted well into the Middle Ages and beyond.

Merlin and Stonehenge

One of the most enduring legends associated with Merlin is his role in the creation of Stonehenge. According to this tale, Stonehenge was originally a circle of healing stones located in Ireland, known as the Giant's Ring or Giant's Round.

The story goes that the fifth-century king Aurelius Ambrosius wanted to create a memorial for British Celtic nobles killed by the Saxons. Merlin suggested using the stones from the Giant's Ring and was tasked with bringing them to Britain. Along with Uther Pendragon (King Arthur's father) and 15,000 men, Merlin journeyed to Ireland, defeated the Irish army, and then used his magical powers to transport the massive stones across the sea.

The oldest known depiction of Stonehenge, dating from the second quarter of the 14th century, shows a giant helping Merlin build the monument.

Interestingly, modern archaeological evidence suggests that the bluestones of Stonehenge may indeed have been transported from Wales, lending a grain of truth to the legend of stones being moved over a great distance.

Connections to Other Myths

Merlin's story shares similarities with other mythological figures from around the world. Like the Greek god Apollo, he has the gift of prophecy. His role as a wise advisor to a king is reminiscent of Odin in Norse mythology or Vishvamitra in Hindu legends.

The idea of a powerful magician trapped by his own magic is a common theme in folklore. It appears in stories from Arabic tales to Native American legends, reflecting universal concerns about the dangers of unchecked power.

Merlin's connection to nature and his ability to talk to animals links him to shamanic traditions found in many cultures. This aspect of his character resonates with Welsh and Celtic beliefs about the interconnectedness of all living things.

The landscape of Wales plays a crucial role in Merlin's story. Many locations in Wales claim a connection to the legendary wizard. Carmarthen, in southwest Wales, proudly calls itself the birthplace of Merlin. The town's Welsh name, Caerfyrddin, means "Merlin's fort."

In north Wales, the mountain Dinas Emrys is said to be where Merlin revealed the fighting dragons to King Vortigern, a key moment in Welsh folklore. The caves and forests of Wales are often associated with Merlin's magical activities and his final disappearance.

These geographical connections highlight how deeply Merlin's legend is woven into the fabric of Welsh culture and identity. The misty mountains, deep forests, and ancient stone circles of Wales provide the perfect backdrop for tales of magic and mystery.

Merlin's story continues to captivate people around the world. From the mists of ancient Welsh legend, he has emerged as an enduring symbol of wisdom, magic, and the mysterious forces that shape our world. His tale reminds us of the power of knowledge, the importance of guidance, and the enduring magic of the Welsh landscape. As long as there are misty hills and ancient forests in Wales, the spirit of Merlin will live on, whispering his secrets to those who listen closely.

Bendigeidfran

In the misty hills and valleys of ancient Wales, where legends whisper on the wind and magic seeps from the very soil, there lived a giant king named Bendigeidfran. His tale is one of love, loyalty, and ultimate sacrifice, woven into the rich tapestry of Welsh mythology. This story, passed down through generations, speaks of a time when giants walked the land and the boundaries between the mortal world and the otherworld were thin as gossamer.

The Tale of Bendigeidfran

Bendigeidfran, whose name means "Blessed Crow," was a giant of a man and the king of Britain. He stood so tall that no house could contain him, and he often waded across the sea between Wales and Ireland as if it were a shallow stream. His sister, Branwen, was as fair as the morning dew, her beauty renowned throughout the land.

One day, Matholwch, the King of Ireland, sailed to Wales to ask for Branwen's hand in marriage. Bendigeidfran, seeing an opportunity for peace between the two kingdoms, agreed to the union. The wedding was a joyous affair, with feasting and merriment that lasted for days.

However, Efnysien, Bendigeidfran's half-brother, was a troublemaker with a heart full of spite. Angry that he hadn't been consulted about the marriage, he mutilated Matholwch's horses in a fit of rage. This act of cruelty threatened to undo the newly forged peace between Wales and Ireland.

To make amends, Bendigeidfran gifted Matholwch with a magical cauldron that could bring the dead back to life. Satisfied with this compensation, Matholwch returned to Ireland with his new bride, Branwen.

Years passed, and Branwen bore Matholwch a son named Gwern. But the Irish court had not forgotten the insult to their king's horses. They began to treat Branwen cruelly, forcing her to work in the kitchens and beating her daily.

Branwen, in her despair, trained a starling to carry a message to her brother. When Bendigeidfran learned of his sister's mistreatment, he gathered a mighty army and set out for Ireland. No ship could carry the giant king, so he waded across the Irish Sea, carrying the fleet on his back.

The Irish, seeing this terrifying sight, retreated inland and destroyed all the bridges across the River Shannon. Bendigeidfran lay across the river, forming a living bridge for his army to cross.

A peace was negotiated, and a great hall was built to honour Bendigeidfran. But Efnysien, still full of malice, discovered Irish soldiers hidden in flour bags, ready to ambush the Welsh. He crushed their skulls with his bare hands.

War broke out, and it was brutal and bloody. The Irish used the magical cauldron to revive their dead soldiers, giving them an endless army. Efnysien, seeking redemption, sacrificed himself by hiding among the Irish dead and destroying the cauldron from within.

In the chaos of battle, a poisoned spear struck Bendigeidfran in the foot. Knowing he was dying, he commanded his seven surviving men to cut off his head and carry it back to Wales. The head remained talking, continuing to speak and keep company with his men for 7 years.

Finally, following Bendigeidfran's instructions, they buried the head at the White Hill in London (now the site of the White Tower of London), facing France. It was said that as long as the head remained buried, Britain would be safe from invasion.

Historical Context and Origins

The tale of Bendigeidfran is part of the Mabinogion, a collection of Welsh prose stories compiled in the 12th and 13th centuries from earlier oral traditions. These stories offer a glimpse into the rich mythology and folklore of medieval Wales, blending elements of Celtic mythology with Arthurian legend.

The story likely has its roots in much older Celtic traditions. The theme of the giant king who becomes a living bridge for his army is found in other Celtic myths, suggesting a common cultural heritage across the Celtic world.

The character of Bendigeidfran himself may have origins in older Welsh or pan-Celtic deities. His name, meaning "Blessed Crow," connects him to the widespread Celtic reverence for ravens and crows as birds of prophecy and war.

The legend takes an intriguing turn with the introduction of King Arthur. It is said that Arthur, in a display of confidence or perhaps hubris, dug up Bendigeidfran's head. He declared that Britain would henceforth be protected by his own great strength, rather than relying on the ancient power of the buried head.

Etymology and Symbolism

The name Bendigeidfran is composed of two Welsh words: "bendigeid," meaning blessed or holy, and "bran," meaning crow or raven. This name carries significant symbolic weight, as ravens were often associated with battle and prophecy in Celtic mythology.

Interestingly, some have attempted to draw connections between this myth and the current practice of keeping ravens at the Tower of London. This link is partly linguistic: in Welsh, "brân" means "crow," while in both Cornish and Irish, "bran" refers to a raven. The presence of the Yeomen Warder Ravenmaster and the carefully tended ravens at the Tower might be seen as a modern echo of the protective power once attributed to Bendigeidfran's buried head.

The magical cauldron in the story is a common motif in Celtic mythology, often representing abundance, rebirth, and the otherworld. Its ability to resurrect the dead echoes themes found in other mythological traditions, such as the Holy Grail in Arthurian legend.

The living head of Bendigeidfran, continuing to speak after death, symbolises the enduring power of wisdom and leadership. It also reflects Celtic beliefs about the head as the seat of the soul and the continuation of consciousness after death.

Superstitions and Beliefs

The burial of Bendigeidfran's head at the White Hill in London was believed to protect Britain from invasion. This belief persisted for centuries, with some versions of the legend claiming that King Arthur later dug up the head, declaring that he would defend Britain by his own strength.

The story also reflects ancient Celtic beliefs about the power of sacrifice for the greater good, as seen in Bendigeidfran's willingness to use his own body as a bridge and Efnysien's self-sacrifice to destroy the cauldron.

The magical cauldron itself was likely connected to pagan Celtic rituals and beliefs about death and rebirth. Similar cauldrons appear in other Welsh and Irish myths, often associated with otherworldly feasts or the restoration of life.

Connections to Other Myths

The tale of Bendigeidfran shares several elements with other mythological traditions:

- The concept of a giant king has parallels in Norse mythology, such as the jotunn (giants) who often interact with the gods.
- The magical cauldron is reminiscent of the cauldron of the Dagda in Irish mythology, which was said to never run empty.

- The living head motif appears in other Celtic stories, such as the legend of Bran the Blessed in Welsh tradition.
- The theme of a king sacrificing himself for his people is found in many mythologies worldwide, including the Norse god Odin's self-sacrifice on Yggdrasil.

Geographical Ties to Wales

The story of Bendigeidfran is deeply rooted in the Welsh landscape. The giant king's ability to wade across the Irish Sea reflects the close ties and conflicts between Wales and Ireland throughout history.

The River Shannon, where Bendigeidfran forms a living bridge, is the longest river in Ireland. While not in Wales, its inclusion in the story demonstrates the intertwined nature of Welsh and Irish mythologies.

The White Hill in London, where Bendigeidfran's head was said to be buried, is now the site of the Tower of London. This connection between Welsh myth and a prominent English landmark highlights the complex relationships between Wales and England over the centuries.

The legend of Bendigeidfran continues to captivate audiences today, offering a window into the beliefs, values, and imagination of ancient Wales. It speaks to timeless themes of loyalty, sacrifice, and the power of wisdom that transcends death. As we retell these stories, we keep alive the rich cultural heritage of Wales, ensuring that the giants of old continue to stride through our collective imagination.

Rhiannon

In ancient Wales, where magic whispered through the air and legends were born, there lived a woman of extraordinary beauty and wit. Her name was Rhiannon, and her story has echoed through the ages, captivating hearts and minds for generations. This tale of love, loss, and redemption is woven into the very fabric of Welsh mythology, a shining thread in the rich tapestry of the Mabinogi.

The Tale of Rhiannon

On a warm summer's day, Pwyll, the prince of Dyfed, sat atop the magical mound of Gorsedd Arberth. As the sun dipped low on the horizon, painting the sky in hues of gold and pink, a sight unlike any other caught his eye. A woman, more beautiful than any he had ever seen, rode towards him on a pure white horse. Her golden hair flowed behind her like a river of sunlight, and her eyes sparkled with an otherworldly gleam.

Pwyll, entranced by her beauty, sent his fastest riders to catch up with her. But no matter how swiftly they galloped, the woman on the white horse remained just out of reach, her pace never quickening beyond a gentle amble. For three days, this strange dance continued, until at last, Pwyll called out to her himself.

"My lady, I beg you, stop for me!"

The woman reined in her horse and turned to face him with a

smile that could melt the coldest heart. "I will gladly stop for you, Prince Pwyll," she said, her voice as melodious as a mountain stream. "Indeed, it would have been kinder if you had asked this of me long ago."

And so Rhiannon revealed herself to Pwyll, explaining that she had come from her own realm seeking him, for she wished to marry him rather than the man to whom she was betrothed, Gwawl ap Clud. Pwyll, already smitten, agreed to meet her in a year's time to make her his wife.

But their path to happiness was not to be smooth. On the day of their wedding feast, a stranger appeared, begging a favour of Pwyll. The prince, bound by the laws of hospitality, agreed without asking the nature of the request. To his horror, the stranger was revealed to be Gwawl, who demanded Rhiannon's hand in marriage.

Clever Rhiannon, however, had a plan. She gave Pwyll a magical bag and instructed him to return to the feast in disguise. When Gwawl was distracted, Pwyll was to throw the bag over him. The plan worked perfectly, and Gwawl found himself trapped inside the bag, at the mercy of Pwyll and his men.

With Gwawl defeated, Pwyll and Rhiannon were free to marry. For three years, they lived in happiness, but a shadow fell over their joy when Rhiannon failed to produce an heir. The people of Dyfed began to mutter that Pwyll should set her aside.

At last, Rhiannon gave birth to a son, but on the night of his birth, the child vanished without a trace. Rhiannon's maids, fearing punishment, smeared puppy blood on the sleeping queen and accused her of eating her own child.

Though Pwyll refused to put Rhiannon to death, he could not ignore the apparent evidence. As punishment, Rhiannon was forced to sit by the castle gate for seven years, telling her story to all who passed and offering to carry them on her back into the castle, like a horse.

It was during this time of penance that the truth came to light. A nobleman named Teyrnon had found the infant on the night of his disappearance, rescuing him from a monstrous claw that was trying to snatch the child through a window. Teyrnon and his wife raised the boy as their own, naming him Gwri Wallt Euryn (Gwri of the Golden Hair).

As the boy grew, his resemblance to Pwyll became unmistakable. Teyrnon, realising the truth, returned the child to his rightful parents. Rhiannon, overjoyed, named him Pryderi, meaning "care" or "loss."

With her name cleared and her family reunited, Rhiannon's tale might have ended here. But fate had more in store for her. Years later, after Pwyll's death, Rhiannon married Manawydan, brother of the British king. Together with Pryderi and his wife Cigfa, they faced new trials when a magical mist descended upon Dyfed, leaving it empty of all people and animals save for themselves.

Through these trials, Rhiannon's strength, wisdom, and magical nature continued to shine, cementing her place as one of the most beloved figures in Welsh mythology.

The Birds of Rhiannon

One of the most intriguing aspects of Rhiannon's legend is her association with magical birds. Known as the Birds of Rhiannon (Adar Rhiannon), these mystical creatures are said to possess extraordinary powers. According to Welsh lore, the song of these birds was so beautiful that it could "wake the dead and lull the living to sleep."

These birds appear in various Welsh tales, including the Second Branch of the Mabinogi and the tale of Culhwch and Olwen. Their ability to transcend the boundaries between life and death hints at Rhiannon's connection to the Otherworld and her possible origins as a goddess of sovereignty and magic.

Historical Context and Origins

Rhiannon's story appears in the First and Third Branches of the Mabinogi, showcasing her as a complex character who embodies both human and divine qualities. Her tale reflects the changing landscape of Welsh society during a time of significant cultural and political shifts, as Norman influence began to reshape the Welsh aristocracy and its traditions.

Many scholars believe that Rhiannon may have her origins in an earlier Celtic goddess, possibly related to the Gaulish horse goddess Epona. This connection is suggested by several elements in her story:

1. Her initial appearance on a white horse
2. Her punishment of carrying people on her back like a horse
3. Her association with birds that have magical powers

The transformation of ancient deities into mortal characters is a common feature in many mythological traditions, often occurring as new religious beliefs overtake older ones. In Rhiannon's case, her story may represent the Christianisation of earlier pagan beliefs, preserving elements of the old religion within a new narrative framework.

Etymology and Symbolism

The name Rhiannon itself is rich with meaning. Derived from the Old Celtic **Rigantona**, it translates to "Great Queen" or "Divine Queen," hinting at her possible divine origins. This etymology links her to concepts of sovereignty and rulership, themes that run throughout her story.

Symbolism abounds in Rhiannon's tale:

- The white horse she rides symbolises purity, magic, and the Otherworld.
- The magical bag used to trap Gwawl represents cunning and the power of wit over brute strength.
- The three birds associated with Rhiannon, said to wake the dead and lull the living to sleep, symbolise the power over life and death, as well as the ability to move between worlds.

The number three, which appears several times in her story (three days of pursuit, three years of marriage before childbirth), is significant in many mythological traditions, often representing completion or divine perfection.

Rhiannon's story is intertwined with several Welsh superstitions and beliefs:

- The magical mound of Gorsedd Arberth was believed to be a place where otherworldly encounters were possible, reflecting the Celtic belief in thin places where the veil between worlds could be crossed.
- The importance of hospitality, as shown in Pwyll's rash promise to Gwawl, was a cornerstone of Welsh society.
- The harsh punishment for infanticide, as seen in Rhiannon's penance, reflects the serious view taken of such crimes in medieval Wales.

Some people in Wales once believed that hearing the sound of hoofbeats with no horse in sight was a sign of Rhiannon passing by, a superstition that lasted well into the modern era in some areas.

Rhiannon's story shares elements with myths from other cultures:

- Her role as a sovereignty goddess is similar to figures like Medb in Irish mythology.
- The false accusation of infanticide is reminiscent of many European folktales.
- Her association with horses links her to other Indo-European horse goddesses, such as the Greek Demeter in her role as a mare goddess.

The theme of the Otherworldly woman who chooses a mortal lover is common in Celtic mythology, seen also in stories like that of the Irish Étaín.

Rhiannon's story is deeply tied to the Welsh landscape, particularly to Dyfed in southwest Wales. The magical mound of Gorsedd Arberth is often associated with Narberth in Pembrokeshire, linking the mythical tale to real geographical locations.

The emptying of Dyfed in the Third Branch of the Mabinogi might reflect historical events such as plague or invasion, woven into the mythical narrative. This grounding of supernatural events in familiar locations is a common feature of Welsh folklore, blending the magical and the mundane in a way that made these stories feel immediate and relevant to their audiences.

Rhiannon's tale continues to captivate audiences today, its themes of love, justice, and perseverance resonating across the centuries. From the misty hills of ancient Wales to the pages of modern literature and the lyrics of popular songs, Rhiannon lives on, a testament to the enduring power of Welsh mythology. Her story reminds us of the strength found in cleverness and patience, the importance of truth and loyalty, and the magical possibilities that exist just beyond the veil of our everyday world.

Mari Lwyd

In the dark, frosty nights of midwinter Wales, an eerie sight once roamed the streets. A horse's skull, adorned with ribbons and glass eyes, bobbed through villages atop a pole. Beneath a white sheet, unseen hands made the jaws clack and the eyes roll. This was the Mari Lwyd, a centuries-old custom that brought both fear and festivity to Welsh communities.

The Tale of the Mari Lwyd

As the year drew to a close, villagers in South Wales would brace themselves for an unusual visitor. The Mari Lwyd, or 'Grey Mare', was no ordinary guest. It was a horse's skull, mounted on a pole and draped with a white sheet. Ribbons adorned its mane, and glass marbles served as eerily lifelike eyes.

A group of men would carry the Mari Lwyd from house to house. Hidden beneath the sheet, one man controlled the horse's movements, making its jaws snap open and shut with a rope. The rest of the group included colourful characters like Punch and Judy, adding to the spectacle.

As they approached each house, the group would burst into song, demanding entry. The householders, prepared for this annual visit, would respond in kind. This musical battle of wits, known as pwnco, could last for hours. Verses flew back and forth, each side trying to outdo the other with clever rhymes and witty insults.

"Let us in, we're cold and weary!" the Mari Lwyd party might sing.

"Not by the hairs on our chinny chin chins!" the householders would reply, borrowing from fairy tales.

This lyrical duel would continue until one side ran out of verses. Usually, the householders would eventually give in, allowing the Mari Lwyd and its entourage inside. Once admitted, the group would be treated to food and drink, filling the house with music, laughter, and the clacking of the horse's jaws.

The Mari Lwyd's visit was believed to bring good luck for the coming year. However, its ghostly appearance also sparked fear, especially among children. The sight of a horse's skull with glowing eyes, moving as if alive, was both thrilling and terrifying.

As dawn approached, the Mari Lwyd would move on, leaving behind bemused householders and a trail of songs and laughter. The custom would continue night after night, sometimes lasting from Christmas Eve until Twelfth Night, ensuring that the whole community had a chance to participate in this unique Welsh tradition.

Historical Context and Origins

The Mari Lwyd tradition is a fascinating piece of Welsh folklore, with roots that stretch back centuries. The earliest written record of the custom dates to 1800, but its origins likely go back much further.

The practice was primarily associated with the counties of Glamorgan and Monmouthshire in South Wales. These areas, with their rich mining heritage and strong community bonds, provided the perfect backdrop for such a lively tradition.

Scholars have debated the origins of the Mari Lwyd for years. Some, like the folklorist Iorwerth C. Peate, suggested a connection to Christian traditions. They argued that 'Mari Lwyd' could be translated as 'Holy Mary', linking the custom to the Virgin Mary. This theory points to the possibility of the Mari Lwyd being a Christianised version of an older, pagan ritual.

Others, like E. C. Cawte, interpret 'Mari Lwyd' more literally as 'Grey Mare'. This view focuses on the physical appearance of the horse skull and its ghostly white shroud. It aligns the Mari Lwyd with other horse-based customs found across Britain and Europe.

The truth may lie somewhere in between. The Mari Lwyd likely evolved from medieval hobby horse traditions, which were common across Britain. These customs often involved people dressing up as or impersonating horses during festivals and processions.

The wassailing aspect of the Mari Lwyd - going from house to house, singing for food and drink - is also found in many British traditions. Wassailing was a common practice in agricultural communities, believed to ensure a good harvest in the coming year.

During the 19th century, the Mari Lwyd tradition flourished in the close-knit mining communities of South Wales. It provided a welcome break from the harsh realities of industrial life and strengthened community bonds.

However, the custom began to decline in the early 20th century. This was partly due to opposition from some Christian clergy, who saw it as a pagan or unseemly practice. Changing social conditions also played a role. As communities changed and traditional ways of life altered, many old customs fell by the wayside.

But the Mari Lwyd proved resilient. In the mid-to-late 20th century, there was a revival of interest in Welsh traditions. Places like Llangynwyd saw the custom brought back to life, often with a new, more family-friendly approach.

Etymology and Symbolism

The name 'Mari Lwyd' itself is a subject of debate among scholars. The two main interpretations offer different insights into the custom's symbolism.

The 'Holy Mary' interpretation links the Mari Lwyd to Christian traditions. It suggests a connection to the donkey that carried Mary to Bethlehem, or to pre-Reformation veneration of Mary. This view sees the Mari Lwyd as a blend of Christian and pagan elements, common in many folk customs.

The 'Grey Mare' interpretation focuses on the horse aspect. Horses have been important in Welsh culture for centuries, featuring in many myths and legends. The grey colour could symbolise the liminal nature of the Mari Lwyd - neither fully alive nor dead, much like the spirits believed to roam during the midwinter period.

The horse's skull itself is rich in symbolism. In many cultures, the horse is associated with travel between worlds. A skull, representing death, combined with lively movement and song, creates a powerful symbol of the cycle of death and rebirth associated with the turning of the year.

The white sheet draped over the Mari Lwyd adds to its ghostly appearance. White is often associated with the otherworld in Celtic traditions. The sheet also serves to hide the human operator, enhancing the illusion of a supernatural visitor.

The ribbons decorating the Mari Lwyd add a festive touch to the otherwise macabre figure. They may represent the Welsh love of music and poetry, both crucial elements of the Mari Lwyd tradition.

The call-and-response singing, or pwnco, is symbolic of the battle between the old year and the new. It also represents the Welsh love of wordplay and verbal contests, which has roots in ancient bardic traditions.

Superstitions and Beliefs

The Mari Lwyd tradition was wrapped in various superstitions and beliefs. Many people believed that allowing the Mari Lwyd into their homes would bring good luck for the coming year. This belief was common in wassailing traditions across Britain, where the visiting wassailers were seen as bringers of good fortune.

Some saw the Mari Lwyd as a way of warding off evil spirits. The midwinter period, when the Mari Lwyd would appear, was often seen as a time when the veil between worlds was thin. The frightening appearance of the Mari Lwyd might have been believed to scare away any malevolent spirits lurking about.

There were also those who saw the Mari Lwyd as a fertility symbol. The horse, in many cultures, is associated with fertility and virility. The tradition of the Mari Lwyd visiting homes could have been seen as a way of ensuring fertility for both the land and the people in the coming year.

The food and drink given to the Mari Lwyd party were not just refreshments. They were often seen as offerings, ensuring prosperity and plenty in the months to come. This links the Mari Lwyd to other midwinter customs focused on securing blessings for the new year.

Some people believed that refusing entry to the Mari Lwyd could bring bad luck. This belief helped ensure that most households participated in the custom, maintaining community cohesion.

In some areas, it was believed that the last house visited by the Mari Lwyd would have special luck. This sometimes led to competition among households to be the final stop on the Mari Lwyd's journey.

The Mari Lwyd is part of a wider family of horse-based customs found across Europe. In Ireland, a similar tradition called the Láir Bhán (White Mare) existed. On the Isle of Man, the Laare Vane (White Mare) was part of New Year celebrations.

These customs share common elements with the Mari Lwyd: the use of a horse figure, often white in colour, and association with winter festivities. This suggests a shared Celtic heritage or similar responses to the midwinter season across different cultures.

The hobby horse traditions of England, such as the Padstow 'Obby 'Oss in Cornwall, also bear similarities to the Mari Lwyd. While these customs often take place in spring rather than winter, they involve horse figures and processional elements.

The call-and-response singing of the Mari Lwyd has parallels in other British wassailing traditions. In England and Scotland, wassailers would sing at the doors of houses, exchanging songs for food and drink. The Welsh pwnco, however, developed into a more complex battle of wits.

The Mari Lwyd's appearance during the midwinter period links it to other customs marking the turning of the year. From the Roman Saturnalia to the British tradition of mummers plays, midwinter has long been a time for reversal of normal social orders and supernatural visitations.

The use of animal skulls in rituals and customs is found in

many cultures worldwide. From the bull skulls used in Minoan Crete to the horse skulls buried under houses in parts of Britain for acoustic purposes, animal remains have long held ritual significance.

The Mari Lwyd holds a special place in Welsh cultural identity. It represents a blend of the ancient and the playful, the spiritual and the social, that characterises much of Welsh tradition.

In the late 20th and early 21st centuries, the Mari Lwyd has experienced a revival. New versions of the custom have sprung up in places like Caerphilly and Llantrisant. These modern interpretations often make the tradition more inclusive, involving the whole community rather than just groups of men.

The Mari Lwyd has inspired Welsh artists across various media. The poet Vernon Watkins wrote evocatively about the tradition, capturing its eerie beauty. Painters like Clive Hicks-Jenkins have depicted the Mari Lwyd, bringing its striking visual aspect to new audiences.

The custom has also found a place in larger cultural events. During the Millennium celebrations in Aberystwyth, a giant Mari Lwyd puppet paraded through the streets. In Chepstow, an annual Mari Lwyd gathering brings together Mari Lwyds from across Wales and beyond.

Today, the Mari Lwyd serves as a potent symbol of Welsh heritage. It represents the endurance of folk traditions and the ability of communities to adapt ancient customs to modern times. The Mari Lwyd reminds us of the rich cultural tapestry of Wales, where past and present, myth and reality, intertwine in fascinating ways.

The Mari Lwyd stands as a testament to the enduring power of folk traditions. From its mysterious origins to its modern revivals, it has captured the imagination of generations of Welsh people. It embodies the Welsh love of poetry, music, and community, while also touching on deeper themes of life, death, and renewal.

As Wales continues to celebrate and reinterpret its heritage, the Mari Lwyd remains a powerful symbol. It reminds us that traditions can evolve and find new relevance, while still connecting us to our past. In the misty valleys and coal-dusted towns of South Wales, the spectral mare still rides, bridging centuries and bringing communities together in song and celebration.